D1784488

MICK CLEARY

RAMPANT PRIDE

THE LIONS IN AUSTRALIA 2013

FOREWORD BY
Sir Ian McGeechan

OPINION QUOTES COMPILED BY
Terry Cooper

EDITED BY
Ian Robertson

PHOTOGRAPHS BY
Getty Images

LENNARD PUBLISHING

Published in the UK in 2013 by
Lennard Publishing, an imprint of
Lennard Associates Ltd, Mackerye End,
Harpenden, Herts AL5 5DR
email: orders@lennardqap.co.uk

Distributed by G2 Entertainment
c/o Orca Book Services
160 Eastern Avenue, Milton Park
Abingdon, OX14 4SB

ISBN: 978-185291-155-3

Production editor: Chris Marshall
Text and cover design: Paul Cooper
The editor is grateful to Georgina Robinson of *The Sydney Morning Herald*
for her contribution to this book
and also to Jake McHugh at the the Grand Hyatt Hotel, Hong Kong,
and Vivian Cooper for their editorial assistance.

Printed and bound in the UK
by Butler, Tanner and Dennis

PICTURE ACKNOWLEDGEMENTS

The publishers would like to thanks the following photographers at Getty Images whose pictures have been used in this book:
Scott Barbour, Tom Crock, Victor Fraile, Paul Gilham, Chris Hyde, Bradley Kanaris, Saeed Khan, Mark King, Mark Kolbe,
Philippe Lopez, Mark Metcalfe, David Rogers, Tom Shaw, Cameron Spencer, Brendon Thorne, William West, Greg Wood.
The publishers are also grateful to AFP for the use of pictures supplied through Getty Images.

CONTENTS

ANATOMY *of the* PROFIT.

The hunter must get *under the skin* of his quarry.

Fig. 1: *A healthy* PROFIT. *Or is it?*

Fig. 2: *A taut musculature, the mark of a healthy* PROFIT.

Nose

Skull

Neck vertebrae

Bendy bit

Spine

Ribcage

Even bendier bit

Pelvis

Tail

Hip

End of tail

Knee

Ankle

Fig. 3: *A sturdy bone structure with no hidden weaknesses.*

Toes

Fig. 4: *Good vision points to a bright future.*

Fig. 5: *A firm footing for stability.*

If you'd like to get under the skin of Profits and Profit Hunting, speak to your financial adviser. Alternatively contact us on the details below. Please remember that past performance should not be seen as a guide to future performance. The value of any investment and any income from it can fall as well as rise as a result of market and currency fluctuations and you may not get back the amount originally invested.

ARTEMIS
The PROFIT Hunter

0800 092 2051   *investorsupport@artemisfunds.com*   *artemis.co.uk*

Issued by Artemis Fund Managers Limited which is authorised and regulated by the Financial Conduct Authority (www.fca.org.uk), 25 The North Colonn, Canary Wharf, London E14 5HS. For your protection calls are usually recorded.

Thanks To Our Sponsors

GREENE KING

I am delighted to say that Greene King has supported the 2013 Lions Tour with jacket cover sponsorship. My association with Greene King goes back a long way and I like to think I have even had a tiny influence on the company. On a golf trip to Scotland I introduced the Greene King team to a pint of Belhaven at Loch Lomond Golf Club and they were so impressed that shortly afterwards they bought the Belhaven Brewery.

Greene King is a great supporter of rugby in general as well as supporting rugby books. After three losing Lions Tours in 2001, 2005 and 2009, it is a very special bonus that this time Greene King has been involved with a superb record-breaking tour. At midnight on July 6th we raised a bottle of Old Speckled Hen to toast the Lions.

ARTEMIS INVESTMENT MANAGEMENT LLP

I have enjoyed a long and profitable relationship with Artemis which stretches back to the last successful Lions Tour in 1997 to South Africa. Artemis is the perfect brand to support the Lions because their original approach to advertising is exactly the same as the Lions. They go out hunting for success in a similar way that the Lions go hunting for success every four years in Australia, New Zealand and South Africa. The 2013 Lions won a magnificent series with a glorious flourish in the final Test, scoring four great tries. I am very grateful to Artemis for their jacket cover sponsorship.

Ian Robertson

● **LEFT** Sir Ian McGeechan and Ian Robertson with Georgina Robinson of *The Sydney Morning Herald* who contributed an Australian view at the end of the Test series.

Foreword by Sir Ian McGeechan

JULY 6th 2013 will be enshrined in British & Irish Lions history – alongside four other days in 1971, 1974, 1989 and 1997 – as a day when an outstanding performance won them a Test series. That night in the ANZ Stadium in Sydney I was very privileged to be one of the 30,000 Lions supporters packed into the ground amidst a cauldron of noise, tension, anticipation and excitement to witness one of the greatest and most dramatic Lions Test performances in their very long and distinguished history, which all began in 1888.

It was the best possible way to celebrate the 125th anniversary of the greatest brand in rugby. After three losing Test series in 2001, 2005 and 2009, they delivered one of the most spectacular victories imaginable.

Following their last-minute one-point defeat in the second Test in Melbourne, the Lions went into the third Test as outsiders, but they proved the impossible is, just occasionally, possible. Warren Gatland revamped the pack, adding more weight, more ballast and more power to destroy the Wallaby scrummage and enable the Lions to dominate the breakdown as well.

The result of this forward domination was to give the backs the time and space to create three breathtaking tries in the second half. In the space of seven days between the second and third Tests, Warren Gatland made seven changes to the Test team, including one positional, and three changes to the bench. The revamped squad revitalised the Lions to the remarkable extent that they turned a one-point defeat in Melbourne into a staggering 25-point win in Sydney.

I should add that a large part of the Lions success was the selection of the replacements bench, with all eight coming on in the second half and all eight making a huge impact. With his much-changed bench, Gatland produced a masterstroke.

This book is the story of another great Lions turnaround, of the underdog beating the favourite to win a Test series, adding something special to the 125 years of Lions rugby. What a month. What a team. What a glorious triumph.

The 2013 Pride of Lions made me very, very proud.

Sir Ian McGeechan's Lions Playing Record
1974 Lions to South Africa: played all 4 Tests; won 3, drew 1
1977 Lions to New Zealand: played all 4 Tests; won 1, lost 3

Sir Ian McGeechan's Lions Coaching Record (Tests)

1989 v Australia: won 2, lost 1	1997 v South Africa: won 2, lost 1
1993 v New Zealand: won 1, lost 2	2009 v South Africa: won 1, lost 2

In 2005 v New Zealand, Sir Ian was Midweek Coach under Sir Clive Woodward; won 5, lost 0.

ALWAYS A GREAT MATCH

The Pride Gathers

The 2013 Lions party to Australia was announced at the Hilton London Syon Park Hotel, which sits in the parkland that surrounds Syon House, London home of the Duke of Northumberland. Not far from Twickenham, Syon was once the site of an abbey. King Henry VIII put paid to that, as he did to the father confessor of the nuns housed there, Richard Reynolds, who took exception to Henry's marital shenanigans. Reynolds was executed and part of his body placed on the abbey gateway.

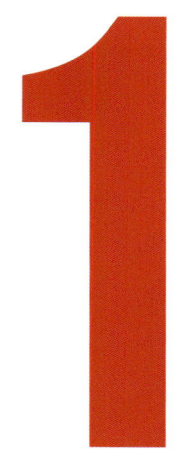

How fitting. There were many who thought that the advent of professionalism in 1995 would see a similar job made of the Lions. No future. No space in schedule. No interest. Off with their heads! Which is why dozens of television wagons arrived with all their paraphernalia, and scores of journalists, and all those others who do funny stuff on the Internet which is supposed to be the future of the media game, shuffled in to take their places among a gaggle of corporate suits and sundry helpers one fair late-April morning to hear tour manager Andy Irvine read out the names of the lucky few – well, 37 – who had been invited to tour Australia. Yes, the place was packed, there was a tingle in the air and if you weren't actually present on site then you were sitting near a television screen somewhere in Britain or Ireland or beyond to take in the live broadcast of the announcement. As we filed into the vast room prior to the formal declaration, someone mentioned that 'the Lions were almost trending worldwide on Twitter'. Apparently, that is a good thing. No, there never was much chance of the Lions going the way of poor old Richard Reynolds.

Irvine himself acknowledged that fact as he did his preamble up on stage, flanked by the coaches and management team. It was glitzy and it was slick. True, that is not to everyone's liking. Some feel that the Lions has become too much of a brand and not enough of a sporting entity. It is too corporate, too driven by the quest for big bucks, and not imbued with the nostalgic feel of old. Well, it's a view. The reality is that with huge logistics to cater for – with back-up staff featuring medics, physios, analysts,

● ABOVE Head coach Warren Gatland, captain Sam Warburton and mascot 'Bil' (British & Irish Lions) after the announcement of the squad for the 2013 tour to Australia. Bil would soon be entrusted to Stuart Hogg as the youngest member of the party.

conditioners, kit men, bag men, Tom Cobley's relatives – it is quite an expedition.

It needs money to make it all come together. And this tour was to be the most financially buoyant of them all. *The Daily Telegraph* reported that the tour was to be the most costly in the Lions' 125-year history, up £4 million from the previous tour to South Africa in 2009. However, Lions chief executive John Feehan had worked the various corridors to come up with a portfolio of sponsors and backers to generate a 30 per cent increase in revenues. It was hoped that the tour would deliver record profits, with some £4 million to be redistributed to the Home Unions. That should keep them happy.

'We hope to achieve what we expected to achieve which is a reasonable distribution to each of the unions after the tour, which will be higher than last time,' Feehan told the *Telegraph*. 'There is no question it will be the most profitable tour but it will also be the most expensive. It will probably cost around £14 million to run the tour. Part of my job is to make sure they have everything they need to make the tour successful.'

The newspaper reported that the players' basic tour fee was £45,000, a figure that would rise to £67,000 if the Lions won all of their matches, including three Tests against the Wallabies, an 18 per cent improvement from the tour four years ago. Salaries amounted to almost half the tour costs, while the four Home Unions were set to receive a fee of £50,000 for each player they provided to the squad as compensation for their unavailability for each country's summer tour, which will cost the Lions a further £1.85 million. The cost of insurance for the tour also exceeded £1 million, while kitting out the 37-man touring party cost £400,000.

So much for the boring, if necessary, detail. You can see why some might rail about the encroachment of finance on romance. Yet as the clan gathered at Syon Park a few weeks later for kitting-out day, it was still possible to detect that evocative air of a Lions tour, one memorably

● FACING PAGE **Former Scotland international Andy Irvine, tour manager for 2013 and a Lion as a player in 1974 (South Africa), 1977 (New Zealand) and 1980 (South Africa), reads out the names of the select 37 chosen for the tour.**

described by former *Times* golf correspondent John Hopkins as 'a cross between a medieval crusade and a school outing'. There was laughter, nervousness, shyness, reticence – all wrapped up in a deadly and earnest intent. As long as the players remain at the core, as long as sport is the centrepiece of every working day, and as long as the famous red shirt is seen as the emblem of a proud heritage and not merely as a photo opportunity, then the Lions will retain the right balance.

That much was evident from the anxiety that attended the squad announcement. There was the usual gamut of emotions to take in. Great pride in the Warburton household as Sam was named captain of the Lions, a secret that he had somehow managed to keep to himself for the preceding eight or nine days, hoodwinking team-mates never mind journalists. Warren Gatland knew his man well. Others may have thought that Warburton had wobbled during the course of the season. Gatland didn't. He knew the inner Warburton to be tough and resilient. Gatland took no notice of those who wondered whether the player's rejection of an offer to take up the Wales captaincy for the final game of the Six Nations Championship would count against him. Warburton had been injured early in the tournament and the armband had passed to Ryan Jones. He in turn had taken a knock. 'Want to lead out the team at the Millennium Stadium against England, Sam?' He demurred, wanting to focus on his game. Gethin Jenkins took over and a famous victory was nailed.

Would Martin Johnson have reacted in the same way? Or the two previous Lions captains, Paul O'Connell and Brian O'Driscoll? No, they would not. But Gatland saw Warburton's decision as a sign of strength not as one of weakness. Warburton had the conviction to speak his mind, to do what he considered to be the best for the team in that he was doing what was best for him as a player. Warburton is a solid character, down-to-earth and without ego. He is his own man, resolutely so. He could have led Wales that day and would almost certainly have been hailed the length and breadth of the land as the captain who stuffed the English. Plaudits do not interest him. Performance does. Gatland had got the right man.

Of course, he would have strong lieutenants alongside, notably O'Connell and O'Driscoll. They would guide him through any choppy waters. The two were part of an initial nine-strong contingent from Ireland, both relieved to have made the plane. O'Driscoll took nothing for granted, even though he had already played a central part in three previous Lions tours. His body was not what it was, but his mind was as steely as ever. He got the nod. O'Connell had had an anxious race against time to recover from injury. He knew that he would be back playing by April. What he did not know was whether he would have enough game time in the locker to persuade Gatland that the force was still with him. It

was. One look at his performance for Munster in their surprise win over Harlequins in the Heineken Cup quarter-finals was enough to prove that.

There were surprises in selection, though. Not many would have thought to overlook Ireland and Ulster hooker Rory Best, but Gatland did, opting instead for a brace of Englishmen in Tom Youngs and Dylan Hartley, along with Richard Hibbard of Wales. That was soon to change, of course, with Hartley's brain-melt at Twickenham, which saw him

● BELOW 'A cross between a medieval crusade and a school outing' – that Lions tour feeling is in the air as the players assemble at Syon Park on kitting-out day.

● ABOVE Brian O'Driscoll would be making his fourth Lions tour as a player. Only two other players (both Irish) had done that: Willie John McBride and Mike Gibson – indeed, they made five.
● RIGHT A look at what happened last time – O'Driscoll beats Joe Roff to run in a try from halfway during the first Test at the Gabba in Brisbane, 30 June 2001.

sent off in the Aviva Premiership final against Leicester for abusing referee Wayne Barnes. Hartley was banned for 11 weeks. The memory of his stupidity and what it cost him will last a lifetime.

Best's initial disappointment was echoed in various other places that Tuesday morning. No Chris Robshaw. No Kelly Brown. No Brad Barritt or Chris Ashton. No Danny Care. The casualty list took on an English hue. Yet they managed to get nine players on

the plane. One man's loss is another man's opportunity, as no doubt Matt Stevens and Mako Vunipola were thinking. The Saracens props were not to the fore in pundits' selections, certainly not Stevens, who had retired from international rugby nine months earlier with a view to spending more time with his young family. A call from the deep blue yonder in early March alerted him to the fact that he was being mentioned in despatches. It was some comeback from the dark days when his life as well as career was spiralling out of control.

Durban-born Stevens is a bright, even-handed kind of guy, a graduate of Bath University with a degree in politics and economics, as well as a graduate of the school of life, having served a two-year ban (2009-11) for cocaine use. The mixed-up kid who dabbled with dangerous habits is long gone. There are those who think he ought to be spending his entire time elsewhere after bringing shame on the game as well as himself with his recreational drug abuse.

'I can completely understand that point of view,' said Stevens. 'But what can I do about it? It would only bring you down to worry about it. My responsibility is to the rest of the squad, my only duty to work my butt off for them. To get hung up on how people perceive you is to go into a downward spiral.'

The Australian press greeted his selection in typically understated fashion with reference to Stevens as 'a South African busted for cocaine'. Another balanced headline spoke of Warren Gatland picking 'slabs of raw, red meat'.

'Well, I'm that all right,' said Stevens, who now tops the scales at 20st 7lb (130kg). 'I'm a big man with a big frame. It's not just about weight, it's what you do with it. As for the Lions, it wasn't on my radar when I stopped playing for England.'

Conor Murray won the nod as third scrum half, Dan Lydiate, only just back from injury, got the vote in the back row ahead of Robshaw and others. Scotland ended up with three players – full back

● LEFT **Prop Matt Stevens in action for Saracens against Racing Métro during the 2012-13 Heineken Cup. Stevens retired from international rugby in August 2012 but was called up for the Lions trip to Australia nonetheless.**

● **ABOVE** Sean Maitland runs at the England defence during the 2013 Calcutta Cup match at Twickenham. The wing was one of three Scotland players to make the plane.

● **FACING PAGE** L on on Lion? Jonny Wilkinson of Toulon is downed by Owen Farrell, one of his successors in the England side, as Saracens are defeated in the semi-finals of the Heineken Cup just two days before the Lions squad announcement. In the end Farrell was in, but Wilkinson was not the thirty-eighth man.

● **PAGES 24-25** Lions players warm up during a pre-tour training session at the Vale of Glamorgan.

Stuart Hogg, wing Sean Maitland and lock Richie Gray, who had played little rugby of late.

There are always quibbles round the edges. Gatland knew New Zealand-born Maitland from way back when. He was a typical Kiwi player – clever, reliable and on-message. So no Simon Zebo, who might have brought a bit of devil to that back line.

And no Jonny Wilkinson. The more the former England fly half shuns the spotlight, the more it seeks him out. The Wilkinson question dominated the news agenda in the lead-up to the squad announcement. It did the same on the day. And rumbled on thereafter.

Wilkinson was supposed to be the thirty-eighth man. The Lions had been expected to name a 38-man squad. The list stopped at player number 37. No number 38. Was Wilkinson the missing link? The responses were less than clear-cut.

'Jonny wasn't available,' said Gatland. 'I rang him on Monday to sound him out. I was really impressed with the way he played for Toulon against Saracens. I asked him if he could tour and he said he wasn't available. I wouldn't have made the phone call if it wasn't to offer him a place on the tour. I told him that we wanted everyone on the tour to be on the plane to Hong Kong and he couldn't make that commitment because he's committed to Toulon. He appreciated the call, but he said he's struggling with his body and managing himself week to week. I think physically he would struggle to do a tour.'

There was some smoke and mirrors in play that day as Gatland fielded questions. Why bother leaving it until the day before the announcement to sound out Wilkinson on his availability? His answer would have come as no surprise, so why bother with the question? It only put Wilkinson on the spot – he

was loyal to his Toulon team-mates and to his contract, as well he should be. The Lions would put great store on that sense of kinship. The date of the French Top 14 final was 1 June, the same day that the Lions would open their tour in Hong Kong against the Barbarians. Of course, Wilkinson could not commit himself.

So two fly halves it was – Jonny Sexton and Owen Farrell. There was a back-up in Stuart Hogg, although no one seemed quite sure just how much rugby the Glasgow full back had played in the No. 10

● ABOVE **Wales and Lions back-row forward Toby Faletau attempts to keep cool by standing in front of water-sprinkling fans as the squad trains in the heat and humidity of Hong Kong on the eve of the tour opener against the Barbarians.**

● FACING PAGE **'Force of nature' Mike Phillips brushes off Barbarians captain Sergio Parisse as the Lions play their first ever fixture on Asian soil. Phillips scored twice in the 59-8 win.**

shirt. The Lions rationalised the decision to go with only two stand-offs on the grounds that the principal playmakers needed to get as much game time as possible. True, but why not give yourselves a safety net by choosing Greig Laidlaw ahead of Conor Murray on the basis that the Scotsman really can fill both half-back roles? The omission of Murray would not have caused undue consternation.

The die was cast. Now all the Lions had to do was get their chosen ones on the plane intact. There were still two big weekends of rugby to go, bone-crunching matches involving 14 players from Leicester, Leinster, Ulster and Northampton. Remarkably, no one got injured. Hartley's wound was entirely self-inflicted. Much as you felt for the man, you could have no sympathy for the player. Discipline is always key and would be with the Lions. Hartley knew the score, so did Gatland.

'Dylan's a young man who has made an unfortunate error,' said Gatland as the players gathered as a complete squad prior to departure from London. 'To play the game you have to play on the edge, but unfortunately he's gone to the edge of the cliff and jumped off it.'

Quite.

The Lions had so little time to get their act together. True, a group of 22 players had been involved in week-long camps at the Vale of Glamorgan in Wales and Carton House in Ireland, so that did give them a foundation as they headed to Hong Kong to prepare for the opening game against the Barbarians. These players would be on duty in testing circumstances, where temperatures were in the low thirties Celsius (high eighties/low nineties Fahrenheit) and humidity was hitting 90 per cent.

The conditions took the Lions by surprise, but they responded quickly. They brought in giant fans to be placed pitchside, the players wore ice-vests at half-time and hydration levels were checked night, noon and morning. The Lions also went to the lengths of getting the IRB to agree to two water breaks being taken in each half. 'It is only common sense when you play in heat such as this,' said assistant coach Andy Farrell on the eve of the match.

Players had been losing seven to nine pounds (three to four kilograms) in training. There is little doubt that there were concerns, the whole issue throwing into sharp relief once again whether it was right that the Lions were in Hong Kong at all.

Not surprisingly, the team itself had a strong Welsh flavour. Nine of the starting XV were from Wales. Even though there was an all-Welsh back row, it did not include tour captain Sam Warburton. He had taken a knock to his knee ten days earlier and had been advised to rest for a week. If it was a blow to him, the side itself was in the very capable hands

of Paul O'Connell, reprising the role he had filled four years earlier in South Africa. There were 17 new Lions in the match-day squad, novices mixed with heavy-duty experience in the form of the likes of Adam Jones, Jamie Roberts, and Mike Phillips.

And the Barbarians? A chastened lot after being hammered 40-12 by England the previous weekend. Apparently they had imposed a booze ban.

● BELOW Lock Richie Gray on the charge for the Lions against the Barbarians. The 6ft 9in (2.06m) Gray packed down alongside Paul O'Connell in Hong Kong.
● FACING PAGE Jamie Roberts tangles with Joe Rokocoko. The Wales centre put in an impressive match performance, while the legendary former All Black set up the Baa-Baas only try.

It didn't last much beyond the press conference to judge by pictures tweeted by the players from Happy Valley Races. Still, the Barbarians did offer a bit of snarl in the opening exchanges, hooker Schalk Brits being sent to the sin-bin for a haymaker that landed flush on Owen Farrell. That's the same Owen Farrell who is a Saracens team-mate of Brits, lives a few hundred yards away and plays golf with him every week. Funny old game.

The Barbarians resistance didn't last. What was a run-out became a romp, an unsatisfying one as the players laboured in the conditions. The enforced water breaks didn't help the stop-start nature of the game. It was all too halting, fractured and contrived to lend the occasion any real merit. The stadium,

packed to the rafters for the annual Sevens, was only two-thirds full at 28,643. The disappointing attendance told its own tale.

The Lions did what they had to do, then got the hell out of there. There were several upbeat displays to admire: from two-try Phillips, a force of nature on the field, aggressive and decisive; from No. 8 Toby Faletau and Justin Tipuric – his Welsh pals in the back row – both of whom were outstanding; from

Jamie Roberts, too, in the centre. The three Scots all gave it a rattle and made a favourable impression. As befits a man of his stature, captain Paul O'Connell opened the tour try account with a first-half score, Phillips getting another before the interval.

The Lions stretched clear after the half-time break as you might imagine they would, running out 59-8 winners. This was a serious business for them. Six tries were scored, including a smartly taken couple from Alex Cuthbert. Jonathan Davies, Dan Lydiate and Alun Wyn Jones were the other try scorers. The try of the match, though, came from the

● BELOW Captain for the night Paul O'Connell gets the tour well and truly under way in sweltering Hong Kong, diving over for the Lions opening try after 28 minutes of the match. It was the Irishman's first try for the Lions, on his twelfth appearance.

Barbarians, scored by Kahn Fotuali'i and created by a dazzling bit of footwork from former All Black wing Joe Rokocoko. It was one of the few genuine moments of class on the night.

Warren Gatland was pleased with the labours. He was not too taken, however, with the minor scuffle that followed Brits's foul play (the hooker was later cited and banned for three matches). Even though

Gatland could understand Owen Farrell's reaction after being hit flush on the jaw, he warned his squad that he would not tolerate retaliation.

'There are times when you need to take one for the team,' said Gatland. 'You can't retaliate because the consequences of your retaliation can be severe as well. We will stress this to the players because there will be times when they are hit or pulled and they have to make sure they don't react to it. It is pretty hard not to react when you are hit square on the jaw but we will emphasise that it is hugely important that the team keeps its discipline. We will be under the microscope a heck of a lot more when we get to Australia.'

And with that, off they went, south to Perth. The real tour awaited.

OPINION Initial Thoughts

■ *SELECTION:*

WARREN GATLAND

Lions head coach Warren Gatland said:

■ *'We spent a long time selecting this squad. There were some close calls. Ultimately we have chosen the squad that will give us the best chance of a series victory.'*

ROB HOWLEY

Backs coach Rob Howley pinpointed the biggest dilemma encountered during the process:

■ *'The decision we spent longest over was whether to take three fly halves or two.'*

● **BELOW** Lions open-side Justin Tipuric runs at Dimitri Yachvili of the Barbarians at Hong Kong Stadium.

■ *DEPARTURE:*

WARREN GATLAND

The disruption caused by Dylan Hartley's suspension and exit from the squad on departure day caused Gatland to issue warnings about self-control:

■ *'Discipline is something I am really strong on. You have to play a confrontational, physical game, operating on the edge without going over it. It's a harsh reminder how important discipline is. You can't do anything stupid or you get a red and find yourself out of the tour.'*

Rory Best was hurried on to the plane and Gatland added:

■ *'Sometimes fate can intervene and a player who was unlucky to miss out has a chance to step up and fight for a place. It would not surprise me if later in the tour he is in contention for a Test spot.'*

The Lions boss made a timely comment about the role of the coaches:

■ *'There's a responsibility on the coaching staff as well to keep a lid on players' discipline and that we don't wind them up too much so that they go beyond the point of no return.'*

■ ***MATCH 1:*** *Lions 59 Barbarians 8, Hong Kong, 1 June*

SIR IAN McGEECHAN

A significant comment was made before the game against the Barbarians by Sir Ian McGeechan, the greatest ever expert on Lions rugby:

■ *'A 30-point win would be good for the Lions – but a 60-pointer would be bad.'*

PAUL O'CONNELL

After the Lions had amassed 59 points against the Barbarians, captain for the day Paul O'Connell said:

■ *'We wore them down in the first half and the points came in the second. The Barbarians are a great side, but mentally they aren't in the same place as us.'*

OWEN FARRELL

Discussing the incident with Schalk Brits, the fly half stated:

■ *'When someone reacts to you, you try not to take a backward step, not just on this occasion, but on every occasion. But you don't want to throw punches. To lose someone to the bin when every game is huge would be massive.'*

Farrell admitted that he had been the instigator:

■ *'I was trying to hold him into a ruck and he reacted. There were no dramas and there was nothing nasty in it. Schalk apologised when he came back on to the pitch.'*

WARREN GATLAND

While urging restraint under provocation after the Schalk Brits–Owen Farrell episode, Gatland was satisfied with the outcome against the Barbarians:

■ *'It was a good run-out, exactly what we wanted. It was our first time together and we did not want to play against a team who had been together for eight months. The momentum puts pressure on the squad for the next game – and that's what a coach wants.*

'It was disappointing to concede a try because we want to be strong in defence. I was really pleased with the platform, particularly off the loose forwards, where Dan

Lydiate worked his socks off and Justin Tipuric again showed what a good footballer he is.'

● **BELOW** A relaxed-looking Warren Gatland talks to the media a couple of days before the tour opener against the Barbarians.

INTRINSIC

Taking pride in giving our clients advice they can trust

Intrinsic is proud of the reputation our national network of financial advisers have built for their integrity and professionalism.

They work hard to understand your goals, aspirations and unique financial circumstances. Intrinsic has the backing of leading organisations in the financial services industry and all Intrinsic services are endorsed by the Intrinsic Customer Promise — that we'll always be fair, open and honest with you.

www.intrinsicfs.com

For financial advice you can trust contact us today on 01793 647400 or visit www.intrinsicfs.com to find your local Intrinsic Adviser.

 SAVINGS

 RETIREMENT PLANNING

 PROTECTION

 MORTGAGES

 ESTATE PLANNING

Proud to be associated with the 2013 British & Irish Lions

Intrinsic, Wakefield House, Aspect Park, Pipers Way, Swindon SN3 1SA

Your home may be repossessed if you do not keep up repayments on your mortgage

On Wallaby Ground

Cloud. 14°C (57°F). Perfect. The Lions could not have been happier than to be bumping their way down to ground level at Perth Airport. They landed at the crack of dawn. It was a typically autumnal morning in these parts – fresh with the thermometer climbing to the low twenties Celsius (high sixties/low seventies Fahrenheit) later in the day. After the steamy, sweaty backdrop of Hong Kong, this was home from home.

A couple of the boys had their boots inspected as they went through customs and immigration. No, not to check the length of their studs in case of fears the local Western Force side might get a shoeing, but to ascertain whether there was any mud on the boots that would contravene environmental controls. Fat chance of getting mud in Hong Kong.

There was a palpable sense of relief in the air as the players checked in to their hotel and got ready for what lay ahead. This was enemy turf, this was where the Test series would be won and lost. This was Australia and these next few weeks would define their sporting lives. This was much better.

The Force were never likely to trouble them too much. The franchise was only in its eighth season.

And they had hardly set Super Rugby alight, commendable as it was to establish a franchise out west. The last time the Lions had been in Perth, in 2001, they had put 116 points on the local side. The Force would be different. But not by much.

In a daft piece of scheduling, the Force were due to play an Aussie derby Super 15 match against the Waratahs four days after they met the Lions. Brilliant. The Lions tour means so much to Australian rugby, filling its coffers with loot from sponsorship deals and the influx of tourists, that it jeopardises its integrity by compromising the fixture list. On the flip side, the Force had had a Super bye the weekend that the Lions were on duty in Hong Kong. Madness all round. Force coach Michael Foley left a stack of front-line players out of the side, doing them a disservice in the process. They will never get that experience back. They were to lose to the Waratahs. Serves them right.

● ABOVE **Danger man. Lions left wing George North in full flight during the 2013 tourists' first match on Australian soil, against Western Force in Perth. The Lions won 69-17.**

● **ABOVE** Now you see it, now you don't. The centre partnership of Brian O'Driscoll and Manu Tuilagi train with Leigh Halfpenny and Jonny Sexton ahead of the match against Western Force.
● **FACING PAGE** 'The guy makes holes wherever he goes.' Well, perhaps not this time, but it still takes three Force players to haul down the fearsome Manu Tuilagi.

There was a dream pairing for the Lions, a potential nightmare for the Western Force, when Manu Tuilagi was chosen alongside Brian O'Driscoll. Tuilagi was selected in the less familiar position of inside centre so as to see how the duo might operate in tandem, with the Leicester man expected to wreak destruction with his powerful ball-carrying, off which O'Driscoll and others could feed. O'Driscoll was handed the captaincy eight years after he first had the honour in New Zealand.

'I'll be following Manu around for the next couple of days just to get used to always being on his shoulder,' said O'Driscoll with a smile and with obvious relish for the prospect of playing alongside him. 'The guy makes holes wherever he goes. He will create opportunities for others by the lines he runs and by the way he carries the ball. He's one threat …'

The others being a back three of George North, Leigh Halfpenny and Tommy Bowe, predators as well as creators all. There was scope in the back line for real carnage.

It was an entirely new line-up as the Lions stuck to their pledge to give everyone a start in the first three games. There were none from the Hong Kong starting XV, with hooker Rory Best one of five new Lions on parade. How Dylan Hartley would have had cause to rue that announcement. There were eight Irishmen in the starting side.

It was not a wholly unsatisfactory experience on the field. The Lions were tested in part, especially up front. But there was a certain inevitability to the outcome, the Lions running in nine tries in a 69-17 victory, six of the tries coming in the second half as the Force tired. The tries were spread around: Sexton, O'Driscoll (2), Croft, Heaslip, Vunipola, Bowe, Farrell and Parling were all on the ledger. There was a tremendous exhibition of goal-kicking from Leigh Halfpenny, who stroked the ball over from all angles with the ease of a golfer on a driving range, effortless and impeccably accurate for 24 points. Halfpenny had been entrusted with the goal-kicking duties ahead of Jonny Sexton, no mean marksman himself. It paid off.

'I don't see being a goal-kicker for the Lions as bringing pressure with it, it's a privilege,' said the self-effacing Halfpenny. 'I love every second of it. I always enjoyed goal-kicking as a kid and I have tried to work hard at it. You watch the likes of Neil Jenkins, Jonny Wilkinson and Dan Carter and you want to be like that. That is up there with the best I've kicked.'

So much for the good news to set alongside signs of a flourishing relationship between Tuilagi and O'Driscoll, the surging power of North and a decent showing from a back row of Tom Croft, Sean O'Brien and Jamie Heaslip.

There was only one story that dominated the night's news agenda and that was an allegation of biting by Lions prop Cian Healy. Force scrum half Brett Sheehan could be heard telling referee Glen Jackson that he had been bitten midway through the first half. Sheehan had been a mouthy presence prior to the game, urging his team-mates to get stuck into the Lions. He is a feisty, gobby, meddlesome figure, like a few scrum halves we can think of.

It was a serious allegation. Biting, alongside gouging, is a heinous act. Sheehan was summoned by citing officer Freek Burger straight after the match to give his version of events. Shortly after midnight, Healy was cited. That was not the only pain that night for the Leinster prop. Shortly after the incident with Sheehan, he collapsed on the turf, screaming in agony and clutching his ankle. Never mind what the disciplinary beaks might do with him, it already looked as if Healy's tour was over.

The hearing was deferred until Friday. The squad had to decamp across the country, a five-hour flight from Perth to Brisbane. Travel is part of the landscape. The Lions had quickly come to terms with that. It would be easy to slip into a mood of self-pity, whingeing and worrying about the strain on the body. You can understand why Clive Woodward sought to do it differently in 2005, locating squads where they were to play and flying in and out of a central base in Auckland. It didn't work. The whole thing was too bloated and

● FACING PAGE Quiet, please. Metronome at work. Leigh Halfpenny lines up a kick in Perth. The Lions full back converted all nine tries plus two penalties for a 100 per cent return.

fractured. It might be stretching a point to suggest that the players enjoy the travel, but they certainly get on with it. Healy hobbled on to the plane on crutches. He knew that this would be the last flight in the company of his newly acquired pals.

So it proved. Healy at least had the satisfaction of being cleared at a four-hour disciplinary hearing in Brisbane. There was no case to answer, the commission decided. Healy was accompanied at the hearing by O'Driscoll, who gave testimony on behalf of his team-mate. It was some consolation at least. Healy was bristling with annoyance that the charge had been levelled.

'I was naturally very disappointed that there was a citing in the first place,' said Healy. 'I always maintained that nothing happened and that I had done nothing illegal. The opposition player's arm hit me. It is as simple as that.'

The gods had been good to the Lions up to this point. They had escaped virtually unscathed from the end-of-season finals, losing only Hartley from the original selection – and that was through his own stupidity. The scales were about to tilt the other way. First Healy, then another loose-head, Gethin Jenkins, who withdrew after being named in the side to face the Reds. Jenkins had been struggling with a calf injury. It had seemingly cleared up. But the curse struck, Jenkins pulled up lame, in went the medics to assess the damage and the hammer blow fell. Jenkins was off the tour without ever having pulled on the shirt in anger. How dispiriting is that, perhaps all the more so given that he had honoured his commitment to the Lions ahead of bench duty for Toulon in the French Top 14 final against Castres.

The two props trotted off into the sunset together that Sunday as their replacements, Alex Corbisiero and Ryan Grant, were winging their way round the world to answer the call. Corbisiero had a mammoth journey, a 40-hour, five-flight stint from Salta, where he had been due to play for England against Argentina that Saturday, via Buenos Aires, Santiago, Auckland and Sydney. It was worth every minute according to Corbisiero, whose season had been wrecked by a knee injury. He had only played a dozen games in 12 months. 'I am going there to be first choice and to put my hand up,' Corbisiero said as he packed his bags in Argentina.

There was more woe to come for the Lions, with an injury to Tommy Bowe in the match against the Queensland Reds. Bowe broke a bone in his hand and his tour also appeared to be at an end. The management decided, however, to cut him some slack until the operation was done. It was a wise move. Rolling with the punches is all part of the experience for a Lions management. Of course losing players is 'a blow', as Gatland said of Bowe's problems post-Queensland. But as one falls, so, in best military fashion, another steps forward. In this case it was to be Bowe's Ireland team-mate Simon Zebo. The tour moves on quickly. In the case of the loose-head props, there was an argument to be made that the Lions had ended up with better technical scrummagers in Corbisero and Grant.

The Queensland game was always likely to be a rip-snorter. How could it not be with Quade Cooper in the opposition ranks, and as captain to boot?

'Quade is a proven winner,' said the Reds coach, former Wallaby prop Ewen McKenzie, a man steeped in Lions lore, having played against them in 1989 and been assistant to Wallaby coach Rod Macqueen in 2001. He tends to know what he is talking about.

'The reality is that we win more games with Quade in the side. But what most people don't know or see is the responsibility and ownership he takes on with regards to our game plan. Right now, with seven current Wallabies unavailable, he is also our most experienced international player.'

The mercurial Cooper was out of favour with the Wallabies and very much in favour with all who cherish instinct over pre-programming, nerve and daring over restraint, danger over caution. Cooper is box office, even if Wallaby coach Robbie Deans doesn't think so. On the eve of the game he pledged to give it a crack and he was to live up to his word.

● LEFT AND FACING PAGE The rough and the smooth. Cian Healy, though cleared in Brisbane of a biting charge from the game in Perth, is to leave the tour after damaging an ankle. Meanwhile, his replacement on the loose-head, a delighted Alex Corbisiero, arrives at Brisbane Airport, having jetted in from Argentina, a journey that entailed five flights.
● PAGES 42-43 Captain Sam Warburton leads the Lions out against the Queensland Reds in Brisbane. A knee injury forced Warburton to wait until the third match to make his Lions debut.

The Lions had selected a mix 'n' match line-up. They refused to categorise what their preferred shadow Test XV was and for that they deserved to be admired. Players respond when there is genuine competition for places. Six more were making their Lions debuts, including tour captain Sam

Warburton. The medics had said that his knee problem was just a knock that needed a bit of time. And that is how it turned out. This was a big moment – for the tour itself as well as for Warburton. No matter how much had been spouted about everyone fighting for his place including the captain, a tour needs a figurehead. You want your leader out there. Warburton certainly thought so himself. He felt incomplete until he pulled on that red shirt and laced those boots.

'A lot of people complicate captaincy and ask me funny questions about it, but I've always just prioritised performance,' said Warburton, packing down with Welsh team-mates Dan Lydiate and Toby Faletau. 'I have a few things that I swear by as a captain – having a positive attitude, developing as a player and building up relationships, being professional and doing my job on the pitch. If I can tick those four boxes then I've done my job.'

He did his job. It was a cracking match, full of bite and thrust, one that engaged the senses for the first time on the tour. The Reds came to play. That much was evident from the very first minute when they ran the ball from their own line. That buccaneering attitude never waned. The Lions had scored 17 tries and 128 points in their two games up to that point. There was never any prospect of them carrying on at such a high-scoring level. This was proper rugby.

Even though they had seven Wallabies away in camp, the Reds could still field nine players with international experience. It showed. There were great match-ups all over the field. It didn't take long for the Reds to show what they were capable of. Owen Farrell had got points on the board for the Lions with his first penalty of the evening. Then the Reds struck – from deep, and hard. Wing Luke Morahan took a ball near his own 22. He swivelled

● **LEFT** Line-out specialist Geoff Parling proved his worth against the Reds, stealing the first two opposition throws.
● **FACING PAGE, TOP** Reds left wing Luke Morahan celebrates his long-range solo try. Three days later, Morahan was called up to the Wallaby squad to replace the injured Joe Tomane.
● **FACING PAGE, BOTTOM** Reds defenders halt Sam Warburton just short of the line after a rampaging run from George North from within the Lions half.

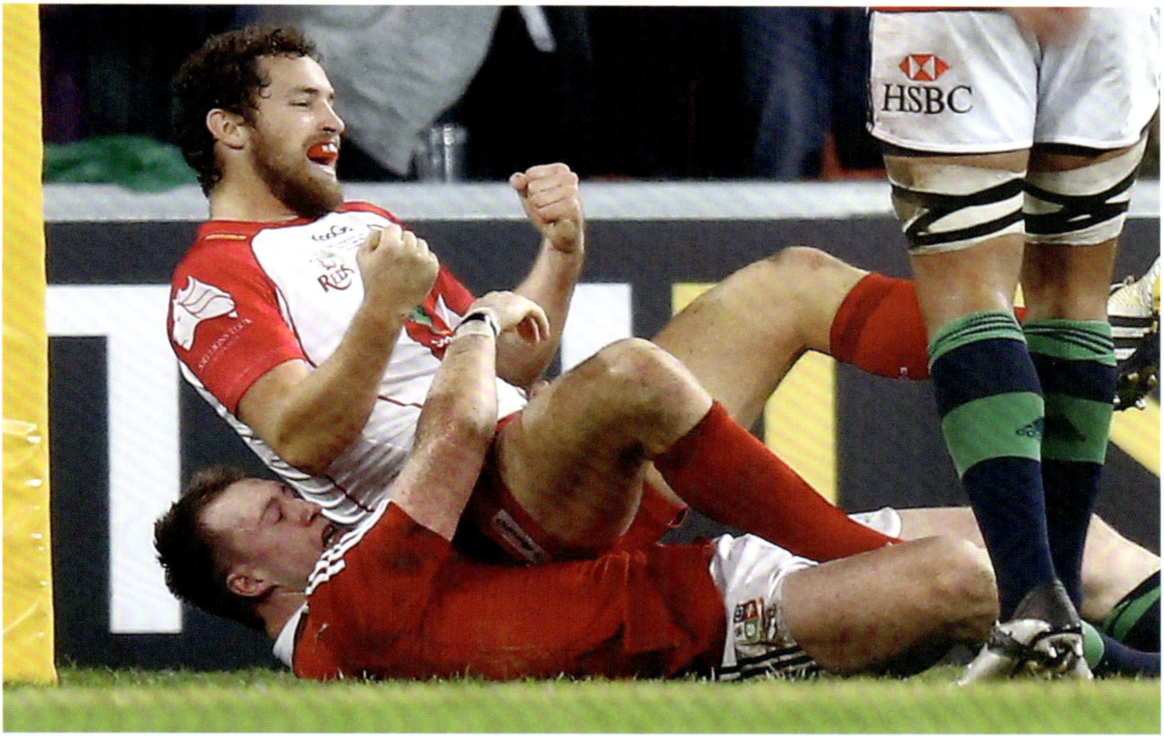
HSBC

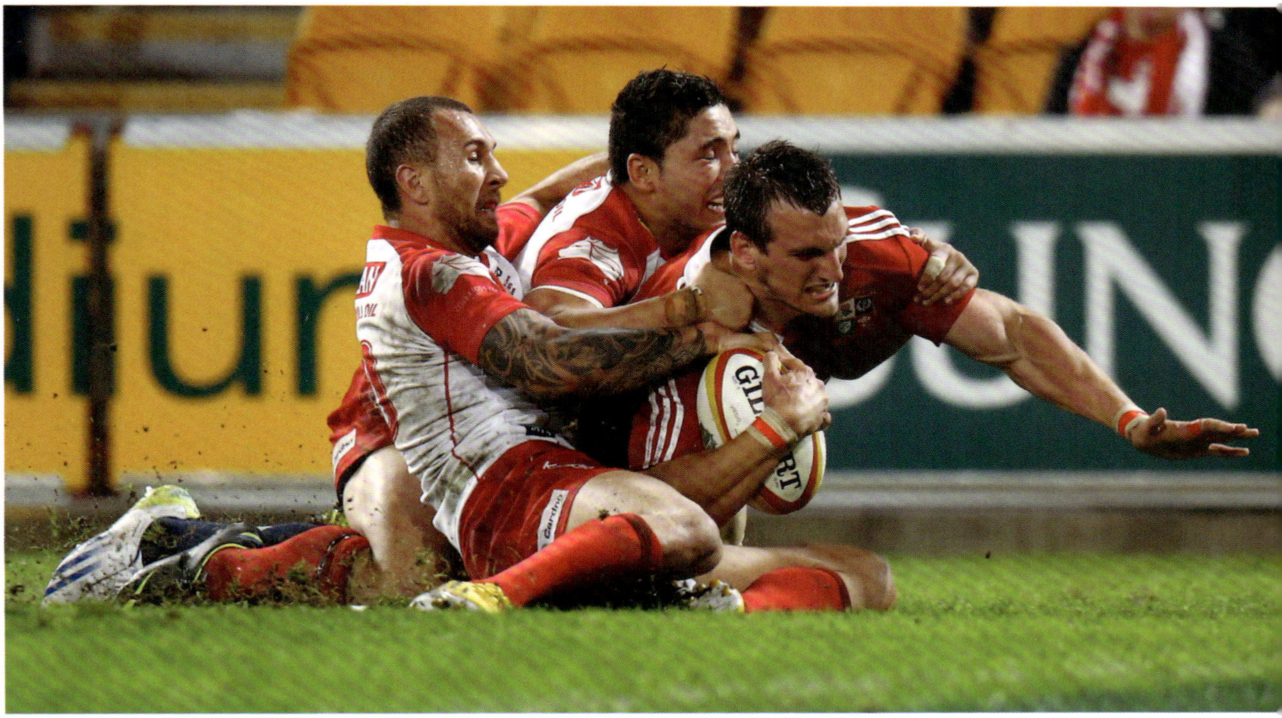

away from Alex Cuthbert, set off upfield, steaming past a couple of Lions, including Warburton who flung out a despairing arm at the disappearing wing, who had Lions full back Stuart Hogg between him and the try line. No problem. A perfectly executed chip-and-gather, and there it was – a sumptuous score.

The Lions, though, did not panic. The pace of the game was frenetic and it could not be sustained. The rains came, too, in the second half, favouring the greater power of the Lions up front. The signs were there from early in the game that they had the edge in the pack. Geoff Parling, on his first start, stole the first two opposition throws. There was always an advantage in the scrummage for the Lions, too. And even though slightly fortuitously, it was through that superiority that they got back into the game on the scoreboard in the 35th minute. Ben Youngs, who had shown well in all aspects, took advantage of a skewed Queensland scrum to hound No. 8 Jake Schatz and fall on the bobbing ball for a try as it squirted out.

The Lions were not restricted to flexing their muscle up front. They went close three times in that first half, with Warburton, Cuthbert and Farrell all denied only by the television match official (TMO).

There was some commanding play from George North, who had come on after only 20 minutes for Manu Tuilagi who had a shoulder 'stinger' injury, as well as from Bowe before disaster befell him. And then there was the goal-kicking. Once again the Lions were without flaw, Farrell hitting six from six for 17 points. The Lions had yet to miss a kick in Australia. On such returns might significant things come to pass.

The Reds kept on coming, but they could not sustain the pace and verve of their opening. They caused the Lions a few jitters with a well-worked try from Nick Frisby midway through the second half, but Farrell settled nerves with his final penalty in the 76th minute. The Saracens fly half answered a few questions on the night about his temperament and poise. He did well. But he is not Sexton, who caused alarms when he came on and then went to the touch line indicating concerns with his hamstring.

The Lions were good value for their 22-12 victory. It had been a proper workout. As ever the focus fell on the injuries. And also on a curious, seemingly throwaway remark by Gatland in the post-match press conference. He was asked an innocuous question about security issues. He replied that the Lions had had to chase away someone from training in Perth who had been videoing them. Gatland also referred to the Australians taking footage from behind the posts during matches, something that was entirely above board.

'Spygate' was top of the agenda for a few days – part froth, part an insight into how noises off can sometimes distract the opposition. Was it a ploy, the question a plant? Gatland denied that it was. But Deans bit and lobbed his twopenn'orth back.

'They create their own stories,' said the Wallaby coach. 'It's just a sideshow really. What the motivation is, you would have to ask Warren. I don't want to fuel the fire. We don't have a security officer, the Lions do. Maybe that's an indication.'

Touché.

Deans was probably glad of the little media storm. It deflected from his decision to overlook Cooper once again. His was not one of the six names added to the squad that gathered at Caloundra on the Sunshine Coast. Kurtley Beale was back in favour after his alcohol-related issues.

The Lions left Brisbane in the rain, buoyed by their results, and headed to Newcastle for the match against the Combined New South Wales-Queensland Country XV. There was a time when these fixtures were part of the real charm of a Lions tour, a visit upcountry to spread the word. They gave the players a taste, or a reminder, of a different style of rugby, rough and rugged, old school. The Combined side were a mix of pros and part-timers, no match for a side of Test players.

You would hope that there remains a place for such games. You fear, though, that they are an anachronism in such a tightly packed schedule. It was not as if the Country boys did not give it a go.

● FACING PAGE Owen Farrell rushes to congratulate half-back partner Ben Youngs after the latter's close-range strike against the Reds.
● PAGES 46-47 In-form Tommy Bowe shows the Queensland Reds defence a clean pair of heels. A broken hand suffered later in the game threatened to derail the Irish wing's tour.

They did, and they kept at it for the full 80 minutes. The Lions, in fact, tailed off, got sloppy themselves. After scoring six tries in the first half, three of them within a five-minute spell to lead 19-0 after just 12 minutes, the Lions took their eye off the ball. The try-scoring was shared around – Alex Cuthbert, Conor Murray, Stuart Hogg, Richard Hibbard and George North with a couple were on the scoresheet by the interval.

North did not appear after the break. He had been feeling his hamstring just prior to the half-time whistle. It was a little injury, but it was to plague him. His replacement, the ever-impressive Leigh Halfpenny, got one of the second-half tries;

● **BELOW** Lions back-rower Sean O'Brien touches down for one of the ten tries racked up by the Lions against a Combined NSW-Queensland Country XV.

● **FACING PAGE** Waratahs coach Michael Cheika was well acquainted with several of the Lions' Irish contingent, having been in charge at Leinster from 2005 to 2010.

O'Driscoll, Sean O'Brien and Jonathan Davies the others. 64-0 was the final score. It was a job done.

The Lions moved on, heading down to Sydney through torrential rain. The weather did little to dampen their mood. As with the Reds, so with the Waratahs. It would be a different order of things, a proper test of their resolve as well as their resources.

There was a familiar figure in the opposition ranks – Michael Cheika, former coach at Leinster and the man who had helped groom several of the Lions contingent, notably Jonny Sexton, Sean O'Brien, Rob Kearney and Cian Healy, all of whom had been nurtured on his watch. Cheika was a typically up-front Aussie coach, happy to trade in banter and gamesmanship. He was looking forward to meeting his old charges. There would be no favours. Quite the opposite. 'I'm disappointed that a couple of them [O'Driscoll and O'Brien] played Tuesday because I would have liked to get a shot on a few of them,' said Cheika. 'Anything in red that moves we'll have a crack at.'

The Waratahs were supposed to be without their entire Wallaby contingent, ten players in all. The criticism that the Australians had received for putting out sub-standard opposition had obviously stung. Two players with the Australian Men's Sevens squad, Bernard Foley and Matt Lucas, were released back, as were, on the eve of the match, two full international players – back-rower Dave Dennis and centre Rob Horne. That was better.

Cheika was adamant that he was not preparing his own side solely for 'a glorious defeat'. He would dearly have liked to have his full retinue available, players such as Adam Ashley-Cooper, Berrick Barnes and the new wunderkind, Israel Folau.

'If we can put some doubt in the minds of the Lions, so that they go into the Test with that doubt, then we are doing our bit to help Australia's cause,' said Cheika. 'We have got to be big. We can't go out just with the hope that we can contain them. We can't hold anything back. We need to put some sort of dent in their tank because it is running pretty quickly at the moment.'

The Lions had need of the Waratahs to be competitive. In an ideal world, a Lions coach would want to run his shadow XV the week before the Test. A Lions tour, of course, rarely runs to desired patterns. As Graham Rowntree remarked, 'This is the sort of gig that you have to make up on the hoof.' How true that was to prove.

Niggling injuries were to shape Gatland's hand. Neither North (hamstring) nor Tuilagi (shoulder) were considered, while it was decided to be prudent with O'Driscoll, who had ricked his hip when chasing a ball against the Combined Country side with typical disregard for his own well-being. The team was to be led by Warburton, but once again

● **ABOVE** Blind-side flanker Tom Croft strides away from the Waratahs to score the Lions' fourth try in Sydney.

● **FACING PAGE** Man of the match Jonathan Davies continued to play himself into Test contention at centre with his display against the Waratahs, which included a hand in four tries and his own name on the scoresheet against the fifth.

Gatland insisted that the captain had to perform and was not guaranteed a Test spot.

O'Driscoll was a pivotal figure for the Lions. Ireland's Tommy Bowe was continuing to rehab from his broken hand. That took to three the number of possible centres out of the selection equation for the following Tuesday's game against the Brumbies, which is why England's Billy Twelvetrees was summoned from Argentina on Wednesday night.

'Ideally you would like to go close to a shadow team,' said Gatland. 'We don't want to pick up any more knocks or injuries. You might need bigger squads in the future. The backs have tended to take most of the punishment, probably because of the

way we have been playing. We have been moving the ball a lot and playing a heck of a lot of rugby. It has taken its toll.'

The forwards had come through pretty well unscathed, but Gatland had yet to nail down his preferred line-up, especially in the back row. Even Warburton was not assured of getting the nod, with Gatland sticking to the line he had been preaching for many months – namely, that Test places would

be determined by form, not by status or carried-over reputation.

'The back-row selection is a headache,' said Gatland. 'Everyone is firing, and if you look at the talent we have there, you saw Sean O'Brien's carrying from 6, and we know he can play 7, we know, too, what talent and ability Tom Croft adds and then there is the devastation defensively and tightness Dan Lydiate can bring. There is great variety among the loose forwards. The two No. 8s also bring different skills to the table. It's going to be a long night making that selection decision. I have been 100 per cent consistent. It is about picking the best players. But Sam is well aware of all this.'

There was heartening news for the Lions in the recovery of their only two specialist fly halves, Jonny Sexton (hamstring) and Owen Farrell (dead leg), both of whom were to feature against the Waratahs, as was Rob Kearney on the bench. The Ireland full back had missed the first four games with a hamstring injury.

The Lions wanted a good old dust-down and they got it. The Sydney Football Stadium had not hit its 40,000 capacity for many years for a Waratahs game. It was full to the rafters for this one. The match lived up to its billing. There was plenty of snarl and niggle, especially around the Lions half backs, Mike Phillips and Jonny Sexton. It is not often that Phillips has turned the other cheek. But he did. He got on with his job. So, too, did Sexton. Well, he did when he was not being pulled and barged, often late, even off-the-ball. Several times Warburton had to speak to referee Jaco Peyper about the orchestrated roughing-up of his players. The Waratahs made no attempt afterwards to pretend otherwise. 'We wanted to give them a good shake around the fringes, get into the 9 and 10, that is where you have got to put the heat on, keep them hopping,' said Cheika. 'Sexton gave me a very dirty look at the end.'

The pair survived, as did most of the others. Most, but not all. The sight of a disconsolate Jamie Roberts limping down the tunnel in the second half with a hamstring injury was a real dark spot on what was an encouraging evening for the Lions as they won 47-17, their biggest ever victory over a New South Wales side. Leigh Halfpenny continued his rich vein of form in scoring 30 points. His usual faultless kicking return of four penalties and four conversions was complemented by two well-taken tries either side of half-time. The haul made him the highest individual points scorer in a match in Australia for the Lions, eclipsing Ronan O'Gara's 26 points against Western Australia in 2001, and was within seven points of the all-time record set by Alan Old on the tour to South Africa in 1974.

Mention of O'Gara evokes memories of the beating he took in this fixture in 2001 from NSW full back Duncan McRae. There was nothing on that scale, but the Lions had to keep tempers in check. And they did.

'There was provocation, they took it to us and they tried to unsettle us with little shoulders and bumps,' said Gatland afterwards. 'We had stressed

● LEFT A storming performance in Sydney from Alun Wyn Jones put him squarely in the frame as second-row partner to Paul O'Connell against the Wallabies in Brisbane.

the need to the players not to respond by losing their head and throwing a punch that might get them banned from the Test match. They were magnificent. We were too big and too powerful for them.'

So they were. The pack was shaping up to be the eight that might do duty in the Tests. There was a powerhouse display from Alun Wyn Jones, who cemented his place in the second row alongside Paul O'Connell. The Welshman was tremendous – hard-nosed, involved and relentless. Good as he was (the pick of the forward pack), Tom Croft ran him close. The Leicester flanker, who feared his entire career was in jeopardy after a neck injury, was dynamic and sharp-heeled, leaving defenders in his wake as he went in for his try in the 54th minute.

It took something to knock those two off the top of the podium for man of the match, but Jonathan Davies managed it. Much as there was woe surrounding Roberts' hamstring injury, the rise to prominence of Davies offset those concerns. The centre was terrific. He had a direct hand in four tries, scored the fifth himself and almost got the Lions off to a rattling start when sending newly arrived Ireland wing Simon Zebo to the corner in the very first minute, only for the touchdown to be ruled out by the TMO for a foot in touch. Davies was a class act. He did all the right things at the right time.

The Lions had to graft hard, but that is what they wanted. In the end, they were so dominant that they were able to see out the final 15 minutes with 14 men, following Roberts' departure.

There was one other thing to record. The Lions had woken that morning to strident claims by World Cup-winning former Wallaby coach Bob Dwyer that they were serial 'cheats' in several aspects of play. Gatland's astonishingly magnanimous response was to sympathise with Dwyer, who had been subjected to a volley of online criticism.

'It is a sad indictment of the media world that Bob has been involved in that and he deserves more respect than that,' said Gatland. 'I find it sad that he should be subjected to abuse now on Twitter.'

The Lions were winning on and off the field.

● RIGHT Jamie Roberts goes down injured in Sydney. The giant centre eventually hobbled from the field, casting doubt on his fitness to face the Wallabies in a week's time.

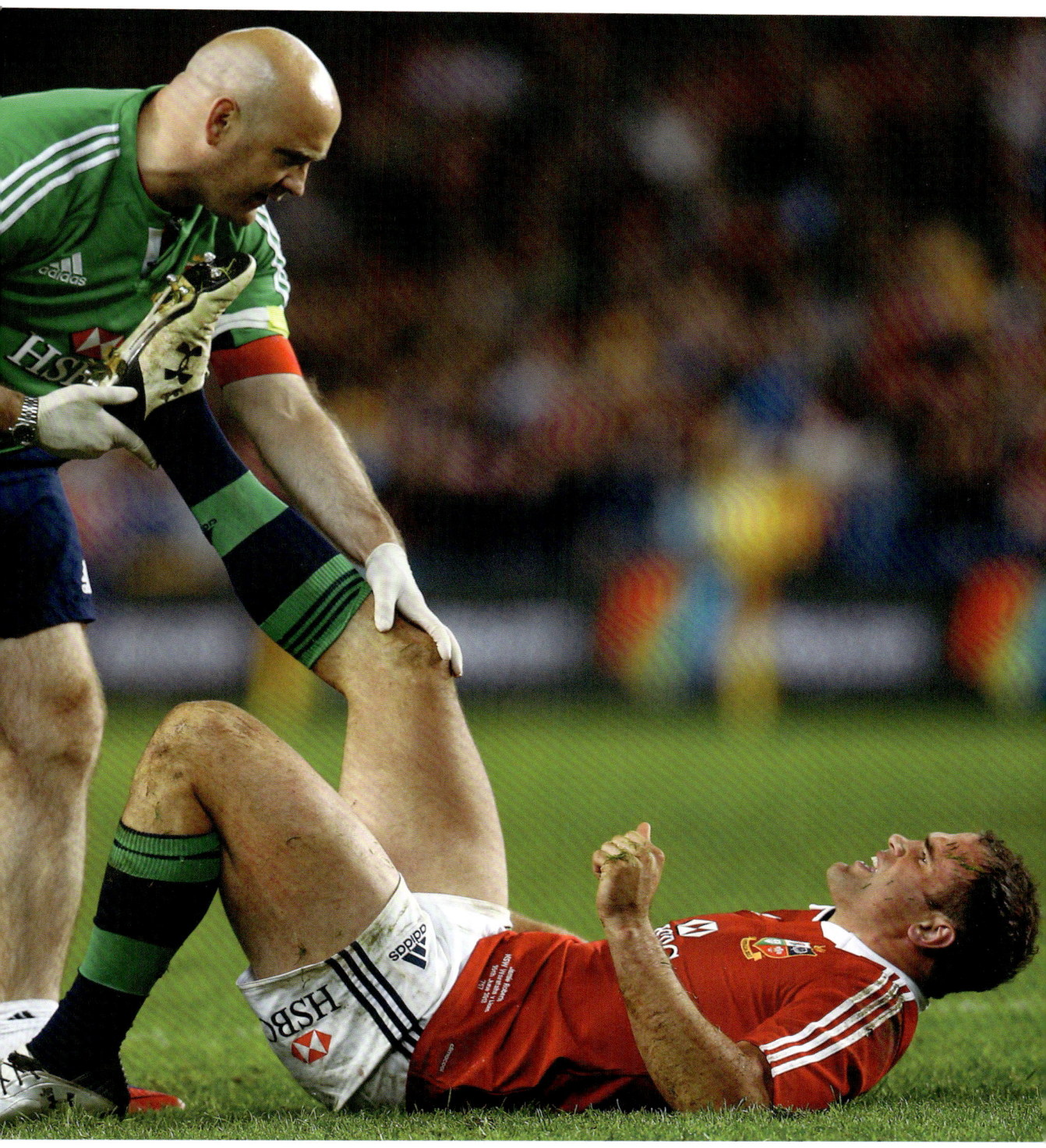

OPINION Matches 2–5

■ **MATCH 2:** *Western Force 17 Lions 69, Perth, 5 June*

LEIGH HALFPENNY

The Lions full back, 11 from 11 from the kicking tee in the Australian tour opener, said:

■ *'I've managed a few, but nowhere as many as that. Sometimes you find that sweet spot early on. I'll take that performance all day.'*

BRIAN O'DRISCOLL

The Lions captain for the day explained:

■ *'There's a lot of brawn in the back line, but there were some subtleties in the mix. I have to thank two big men – George North and Manu Tuilagi – for some nice offloads.'*

■ **MATCH 3:** *Queensland Reds 12 Lions 22, Brisbane, 8 June*

SAM WARBURTON

The tour captain finally got to lead his team out in Brisbane and acknowledged:

■ *'Reds came out red hot, big time. That was a great challenge for us.'*

BEN YOUNGS

Try scorer Youngs praised his pack:

■ *'The scrum was outstanding. Reds chucked everything at us in their first 20 minutes.'*

WARREN GATLAND

The Lions head coach unusually commended individuals from the game against Queensland:

■ *'George North is causing damage and is having a big impact on the tour. Ben Youngs was excellent. He brings subtlety to the game.'*

GEORGE NORTH

The powerful Lions threequarter asserted:

■ *'We don't want to be seen as just physical players. We want finesse and style.'*

QUADE COOPER

The controversial Queensland and Australia fly half said:

■ *'The only way we could get an edge over them was to run them around.'*

■ **MATCH 4:** *Combined Country XV 0 Lions 64, Newcastle, 11 June*

WARREN GATLAND

Gatland was in grim mood after the match:

■ *'There was some excellent stuff and some average stuff.'*

Note: 'Average' is southern-hemisphere speak for 'appalling' and 'terrible'.

BRIAN O'DRISCOLL

Captain once again in the win over the Combined Country, the centre had this to say:

■ *'We should have been able to kick on, but didn't.'*

● **BELOW** Newly arrived wing Simon Zebo, on Lions debut, challenges Cam Crawford of the Waratahs.

● **ABOVE** Having slotted effectively into his reserve role as stand-off, Stuart Hogg, primarily a full back, scored 13 points against the Combined Country, including this try.

ROB HOWLEY

The tourists' backs coach felt the Lions could draw some positives from the performance:

■ *'You lose continuity when you bring players on and that was frustrating. But we're generally happy with ten tries. We are delighted with Stuart Hogg. He played flat and facilitated the centres.'*

■ **MATCH 5:** NSW Waratahs 17 Lions 47, Sydney, 15 June

WARREN GATLAND

Just as after the match in Brisbane, the Lions head coach was once again eager to name the major contributors:

■ *'Alun Wyn Jones was outstanding, showing physicality, presence and ball-carrying – a real cog in the middle of our forwards. Jonathan Davies was very good in midfield, Simon Zebo had a great start and Leigh Halfpenny continued to kick his goals.*

'The performance was out of the top drawer – even with 14 men we still dominated. The scrum was strong and the impact of the bench players was excellent.'

ALUN WYN JONES

A key performer against the Waratahs, the lock commented:

■ *'We were determined to make the most of our chances, especially early on, because there might be few of them. The focus was breakdown, breakdown, breakdown.*

'The tight five don't want to be anonymous. We want to get our hands on the ball.'

JONATHAN DAVIES

The man of the match remarked:

■ *'Part of the midfield's job is to make sure the dangerous back three are put in space. There is a lot of emphasis on giving them the ball.'*

Win or Lose, Celebrate with...

RICKETY BRIDGE

FOUNDED 1797

Rickety Bridge is an historic Franschhoek wine estate, founded in 1797 by the widow Paulina de Villiers, and set in lush vineyards shadowed by the majestic Dassenberg and Wemmershoek Mountains. Cross the 'rickety bridge' into a haven in the vines and revel in this multi-faceted offering of fine wine, delectable cuisine and luxury accommodation.

Today Rickety Bridge is home to a modern boutique winery producing world class wines, a bistro style restaurant, romantic wedding and function venue and a luxurious 4 star guest house set in the original Cape Dutch Manor House.

Its flagship wines, the Paulina's Reserve range, proudly bear the name of the original owner of the property. These are complimented by the Rickety Bridge classic range, and both have received numerous accolades and awards in recent years in recognition of the quality produced by young winemaker Wynand Grobler.

Tel: +27 (0) 21 876 2129 ♣ info@ricketybridge.com ♣ www.ricketybridge.com
R45, Franschhoek, Western Cape, South Africa

First Test

The midweek side. What do you do with them? Ignore them, decide on your Test squad and send the dirt-trackers out each week with a brief to give it a go but not to worry if it goes wrong? Or do you pretend that there is a genuine 'All for one, one for all' spirit at work? Insist that those who turn out midweek are every bit as important as those who pull on the Test jersey? Of course, some of this may be bluff and players see through it all pretty quickly, but at least they might appreciate the facade.

Graham Henry ditched the midweek side early during the 2001 tour to Australia, perhaps even before the 747 had left the tarmac at Heathrow. He did so publicly once they had lost to Australia A at Gosford, stressing that it was all about the Test team from that point on. The players had got there before him. They knew that he had his chosen ones in mind. They were there to make up the numbers. No wonder the tour almost came apart at the seams, as Matt Dawson so graphically outlined in a tour diary in *The Daily Telegraph.*

Four years later, Clive Woodward went at it a different way. He went big, taking a huge number of players and spreading resources so that the midweek boys had their own coaching panel, Ian McGeechan

● ABOVE **Kurtley Beale looks disbelievingly at the shredded turf after slipping and missing a last-minute penalty that would have won the first Test for the Wallabies in Brisbane.**

and Gareth Jenkins. It went well enough in that regard, the midweek side returning a perfect record on what was a pretty abject tour. There was little connection, little esprit de corps.

And this time? Well, as in 2009, the whole group was as one. There was genuine competition for places, the spirit was harmonious, the players backed one another and they bought in to the mantra. Test spots were all on the line. That much was to be seen in the selections up to this point.

And then came Canberra. It was not a happy experience. It was not an easy one either. Gatland took a gamble with his selection. Did it pay off? Well, the midweek side lost 14-12 to the Brumbies, and for long stretches of the first half were hapless and lifeless. It was a performance that did the shirt no credit at all. But what might we have expected? There were injuries in camp and Gatland decided to put his Test players in cotton wool. And how!

No one, but no one, managed to second-guess his decision to summon Shane Williams from Japan to revive what we might loosely call his international career, even though, of course, there are no caps awarded. Williams had called time 18 months earlier, rounding off in suitably dramatic fashion by scoring with his last touch against Australia. When the call came through from Lions attack coach Rob Howley, he thought it was a wind-up. He wasn't the only one. Williams had been due to be in Australia as a summariser for talkSPORT radio. At least his papers were in order.

'If I had any doubt whatsoever that I wasn't capable or good enough then I would have said no, because there is no way I will let the Lions down,' said Williams, who thought he had signed off on his Lions experience when scoring two tries in the last match the side had played in South Africa in 2009, the 28-9 win in the third Test in Johannesburg.

Williams was not the only one in a state of shock that Monday morning at the North Sydney Oval where the makeshift side was being put through its paces ahead of flying to Canberra. The team to face the Brumbies was one of the most hastily cobbled together in the history of the Lions and it was up against Australia's most successful franchise, a team that was already through to that season's Super Rugby play-offs and was coached by one of the shrewdest, most hard-nosed blokes in world rugby, World Cup-winning former Springbok coach Jake White.

Three new kids on the block lined up in the Lions back division: Williams accompanied by Brad Barritt, just arrived from an interrupted holiday in Los Angeles, and Christian Wade, pulled at short notice prior to England's second Test against Argentina in Buenos Aires. Add to the mix Billy Twelvetrees, who by the standards of that madcap Monday must have seemed a veteran tourist despite having arrived from Argentina himself only three days earlier, and this was the threequarter line sent out to face the Brumbies – they had barely shaken hands with each other, let alone trained together.

● LEFT England's Christian Wade and Brad Barritt flank former Wales international Shane Williams. All were called to Australia to provide cover for the Lions' injury-hit back division.

● ABOVE Lions No. 8 Toby Faletau is hauled down by his opposite number, Brumbies skipper Peter Kimlin, who was given leave from the Wallaby training camp to play in the match.

● FACING PAGE Dan Cole leads a disconsolate set of Lions off the pitch in Canberra after their 14-12 defeat by the Brumbies.

Perhaps we should not have expected too much. We certainly didn't get much. True, the build-up had been far from ideal and conditions were tricky in Canberra, with sleet hammering down a couple of hours before kick-off. The Lions, though, ought to have shaped up better. They were abject in the first half, not helped by a terrible line-out performance from their captain, Rory Best. The poor bloke had a public meltdown with his throwing, a case of the yips. Six line outs went begging on his watch alone.

It was a lonely place for the captain, incapable of rousing the troops as his own game fell apart.

The Brumbies were good value for their 14-12 win, despite the narrowness of the margin and the fact that a couple of Stuart Hogg penalties rattled the woodwork. The Lions were well beaten, a late rally when the cavalry came on notwithstanding, the scores closing from 14-3 to within two points as Hogg and then Owen Farrell knocked over penalties. The Lions conceded a soft early try to Tevita Kuridrani, the Brumbies centre, who breezed through flimsy tackling by Wade. That set the tone, with the Brumbies captain, Wallaby forward Peter Kimlin, an abrasive presence.

Did the defeat really matter? Yes, it did, no matter that Gatland had protected his front-line troops. The Lions jersey always has to have meaning and resonance or it means nothing at all. Either the Lions are genuine tourists or they are not. You can't pick and choose in these matters. The defeat was the first to a provincial side in 16 years, the losses to Australia A in 2001 and the Maori in 2005 being to representative sides. It was the first defeat to a regional Aussie side in 42 years. That was the magnitude of the moment.

The Lions had been undefeated. There had been a hint of a swagger about them as they approached the Test series. The Australians had certainly noticed. Gone, all gone.

But just as tours can dip, through defeat or injury, so can they rise. That up and down of a Lions tour is what keeps people engaged. No sooner had the Lions suffered their first setback than they were off the canvas and fighting back. They were given a stern talking-to prior to leaving Canberra and heading to Brisbane, a sharp reminder of what the Lions meant and represented.

The real pick-me-up came with news that wing George North was fit. It was terrific for the Lions, a much-needed boost. Even a few days earlier, Gatland had rated his chances at 'no more than 50-50'. Privately, the medics felt that the giant Scarlets wing, bound for Northampton Saints for the following season, would miss out by a day or two.

Yet, on Wednesday afternoon, as Rob Howley fronted a press conference in the well-appointed surrounds of Tattersall's Club in downtown Brisbane (even the media looked smart – well, most of them), there was no disguising his delight at news that one of the Lions' principal strike runners was available.

'George is a phenomenal athlete,' said Howley. 'We have only seen glimpses of him so far. He has got depth to his game, power and speed. He works tirelessly. When he made his debut against South

● LEFT Former centre Tom Youngs, who converted to hooker in 2009-10 and rose to join brother Ben in the England team, was handed the Lions No. 2 jersey for the first Test.
● FACING PAGE In Brisbane, James O'Connor (here on left with back-row forward Liam Gill) was to make only his second start at fly half for the Wallabies in what would be his thirty-eighth Test.

was to rumble into action, the guns pointed at Wallaby lines.

North's return was a shock in that he had defied medical prognosis. The real surprise in selection was the preference for Alex Corbisiero over Mako Vunipola on the loose head. Corbisiero was not part of the original squad selection and had been summoned only once Cian Healy and Gethin Jenkins went crook. He was a more reliable, accurate scrummager than Vunipola. It was the right call.

Elsewhere, Tom Youngs got the nod over Richard Hibbard at hooker, a reward not just for the vibrancy of his outfield play but also for the smooth mechanics of his game at scrum and line out. The back five was as expected, with Warburton in position on the open side alongside Jamie Heaslip and Tom Croft. The Lions were in good shape.

The Wallabies, too, were giving off positive noises, although there were many eyebrows raised with the choice of James O'Connor at fly half. It was only the second time that he had started there in a Test career stretching back five years. It was a gamble. There were three debutants in the team: Ben Mowen in the back row; the industrious, highly respected Queenslander Christian Leali'ifano at inside centre, the Wallabies looking to have two playmakers in midfield; and then there was Izzy – Israel Folau, the triple-code superstar of Australian sport, a rugby league international and high-grade Aussie Rules footballer. Folau had had fantastic notices in the build-up, about his star quality, his athleticism, his fast feet, his balance and nerve. He was supposed to be the complete package despite having only played 15 matches of union for the Waratahs. Could he live up to the hype? Of course he could.

Folau was the headline act, a new kid to boot with a sexy backstory. But the real motor of the Wallabies was to be found at scrum half in Will Genia. How blessed have the Australians been to

Africa aged 19, he had 21-22 touches. That's what a wing has to do in the modern game, have lots of involvement. It is a huge morale boost for us to have him available, a real fillip. I have never seen him looking in better shape.'

How true that was to prove. North was so important to the whole project, not just as an individual player. North was gold dust: potent, hardworking and a wreaker of havoc, the Lions' most productive player on the trip to that point. His loss would have been a blow, all the more so given that the rest of the Lions back-line heavy artillery – Tommy Bowe, Jamie Roberts and Manu Tuilagi – were all forfeit. The Lions lacked a puncher through that midfield channel. But the tank-like North

have a lineage in such a pivotal position that stretches back in the recent past from Genia through George Gregan to Nick Farr-Jones – three of the greatest players ever to have played the game, never mind just three of the greatest scrum halves. And we have not even linked back to the peerless Ken Catchpole in the 1960s.

Genia, who had missed a chunk of last season through injury was a key man. As was to be proved.

'Will has all the classic skills – a good pass, a good kick and a great defence,' said Farr-Jones. 'He has vision and judgment, too, aware of when to go short or go wide, the whole bag of tricks. He is learning to put his imprint on the game. Will is right up there now at the height of his game. And that game has to come out in its full glory if the Wallabies are to win.'

The backdrop was expected to be raucous and colourful. There had been as much focus on the fans as on the players, as if they were a sixteenth man and could affect the outcome. Well, they did have a significant effect on events in 2001 when they stunned the locals at the Gabba.

The Aussies arrived prepared this time. The Suncorp was the Wallabies' favourite stadium. They had only ever lost to New Zealand there. Mind you, the Lions had played seven times in Brisbane and never lost. In the battle of steel and girders, honours were even.

The supporters flooded into Brisbane on the morning of the match, transforming the city. The stage was set.

The 2013 influx of fans was expected, but it was no less engaging. The locals got in on the act this time and the Suncorp was at its finest. The record 52,499 crowd was not to be disappointed.

The action was fast, dramatic and sustained from first to last. One of the Wallaby new boys, Christian Leali'ifano, was knocked senseless in the very first minute after an accidental collision with the hip of Lions centre Jonathan Davies. He was stretchered off the field. The Wallaby woes did not end there. Player after player went down injured. There had rarely been scenes like it, although the casualty rate from

the second Test in Pretoria four years earlier, when four Lions – two props and two centres – were carted off within minutes of each other in the second half, certainly came close.

● RIGHT Debutant Christian Leali'ifano lies on the Brisbane turf, put out of the game in the first minute by an accidental collision with the hip of Lions centre Jonathan Davies (No. 12).

These injuries were all in the Wallaby back line. Berrick Barnes (head), Pat McCabe (neck), Digby Ioane (shoulder) and Adam Ashley-Cooper (shoulder) all suffered on the night, with Ioane somehow soldiering on only to be ruled out of the series a few days later. By the final whistle, Australia had played a long stretch with a flanker, Michael Hooper, in the centre. Reserve scrum half Nick

Phipps did a late shift there too. Yet for all the disruption, the Wallabies hung in there. In fact, they did far more than that. They had a marvellous chance to win the match with the very last kick of

● BELOW 'The real motor of the Wallabies.' Will Genia prepares to put boot to ball as Lions No. 8 Jamie Heaslip closes in. Genia had a central role in Israel Folau's sensational first score.

● FACING PAGE Triple-code wunderkind Izzy Folau celebrates his first try for the Wallabies with Adam Ashley-Cooper (No. 13).

● PAGES 70-71 Wallaby prop Benn Robinson offloads as he is caught by Paul O'Connell of the Lions during the first Test.

the game, only for Kurtley Beale to fluff the opportunity by slipping as he attempted the penalty from 47 metres. The ball skewed low to the left and the roars erupted from the red hordes in the stands.

They had all been treated to a humdinger of a Test match, a proper examination of skill as well as nerve. There was a stunning debut from Israel Folau to embrace, the star of league, Rules and now union showing just what all the fuss had been about. There was a crackle every time the ball came near him and there will be a crackle for years to come. He is box office: tall, powerful, dynamic with bewitching feet.

It did not take long for him to get noticed. Referee Chris Pollock, as he did several times on the evening, made an unfathomable decision to end a penalty advantage to the Lions in the Wallaby 22, even though they had only rumbled through a few phases for no great gain, awarding a penalty to the Wallabies. Will Genia needed no second bidding to strike. He saw the Lions were scrambled, so tapped and went. Folau was alert to it and tracked his man as Genia weaved and raced upfield. The Lions backpedalled but it was too late. They were breached and as they finally closed in on Genia, the scrum half nudged a kick through which Folau latched on to and hotfooted it to the line.

It was a sensational score, James O'Connor's conversion meaning that there had effectively been a ten-point turnaround in the blink of an eye. There were only 13 minutes gone on the clock. Behind the posts, the Lions drew breath. They had to remain composed despite the shock of the score. If they did not understand how dangerous the Genia-Folau combination could be, they did now. It was a sucker punch and they had to pick themselves off the canvas pretty damn quickly.

They did. All the hokum spouted about bonding and spirit only has meaning at times like these. This is when you need your mates alongside. This is when you need to trust each other.

● **PAGES 74-75 AND ABOVE** George North lives up to his billing as a key Lions weapon. Catching a Wallaby kick in his own half, he left several defenders in his wake on his way to the line.
● **RIGHT** Anything you can do … Israel Folau powers away from Jonny Sexton and Alex Corbisiero to round off his second wonder try of the night.

If the Wallabies had Folau, then the Lions had George North. Anything Folau could do, North could match. There had been so much effort put in to getting North fit, and as the ball dropped into his arms from a poor clearance kick from Barnes in the 23rd minute you could see why. The Lions wing fielded the ball around his own ten-metre line. There was a gaggle of Wallabies in front of him. Within a few seconds there was a gaggle of Wallabies behind him, all stretched out grasping at thin air. Pace, power, confidence – North had the lot as he surged to the try line. Lions centres Davies and O'Driscoll were inside him. He had no need of them, North rounding off in style. Well, apart from the silly finger-pointing gesture directed at Genia as he made a despairing effort to get to him near the try line. North was later to apologise for being a daft pillock. It was out of character. The try was not. The boy is special.

It was that kind of night. Folau edged himself ahead in the superstar stakes with his second score of the evening five minutes before half-time, a real soft-shoe shuffle as he took a ball from Ben Mowen, stepped Jonny Sexton and beat Alex Corbisiero. The stadium roared, as well it might. Even the Lions fans had to tip the hat to that one.

The conversion by O'Connor was missed, a disturbing sign for the Wallabies. Goal-kicking flaws were to cost Australia. They had already missed eight points by this stage, going in to the half-time break at 13-12 down. The Lions closed out the half with a near miss in the corner, the Wallabies conceding a penalty as they tried to stop Davies. It might have been a yellow card against Wycliff Palu, but he got the benefit of the doubt. Leigh Halfpenny, though, missed the kick, a momentous event in itself.

The Lions always had that edge of dominance yet only led by a point. Their scrum was on top of the Wallabies', one churning shunt downfield bringing great cheers from the crowd. They needed to make that advantage count on the scoreboard. Within seven minutes of the restart they had managed that. Again it was a wing who scored. Again it was a wonder try. It was Alex Cuthbert this time getting in on the act. The strapping youngster took a ball from Sexton in midfield, hit the afterburners and charged past a startled defence. Cleverly, the Lions had spotted that Hooper had moved to midfield, and struck hard. There was a brief dampener on their celebrations as the TMO checked for a possible obstruction by O'Driscoll on O'Connor. Try given, conversion nailed, 20-12 to the Lions. They looked to be in a good place.

Yet the Wallabies would not run up the white flag. Still they came at the Lions. Still they strained to get ball through their forwards. And slowly but surely they inched their way back into contention.

O'Connor knocked over a penalty, then so did Beale in the 62nd minute. Halfpenny replied a few minutes later to leave the score at 23-18 to the Lions. Fingernails were being chewed. Back came Beale in the 68th minute. Another successful Beale penalty.

If only that sentence could have been written once more, the Australians would have been in heaven. As it was, two chances went begging, the last of them that dramatic slip after a penalty had been awarded in the 80th minute for a splintering Lions scrum. Beale slipped, the kick missed and the whistle blew. 23-21 to the Lions. Cue bedlam.

It had been a Test packed with incident. There were those who considered the Lions had been lucky. No, they hadn't. True, Australia missed 14 points in all through duff kicks, the last of which was to be replayed endlessly, and the picture of Beale slipping as the Suncorp turf came apart around his sliding boot was splashed across the next day's papers.

But every Lions Test match is made up of micro-moments that matter. The Lions had put a lot of work into their goal-kicking and had a dedicated man in their ranks, Neil Jenkins, to make sure everything, but everything, that could be done to ensure success was done. That included having the right studs. Australia did not have a specialist kicking coach on site. Gatland took a certain relish the following day in pointing out that Beale had been wearing moulded studs.

'If I was a coach looking at Kurtley Beale coming on, I would be looking at the boots he was wearing,' said Gatland. 'He came on to the field wearing "mouldies" and he slipped over taking that last kick. He slipped over on a couple of other occasions. Why has he come out on the field wearing that sort of footwear in those sort of conditions? We've had these issues a lot with our players with Wales in the Millennium Stadium. It's quite a slippery surface and on a lot of occasions we've told players to make sure they have the right footwear because it is a slippery surface and you have to turn up with the right tools. It's part of your job making sure that you are prepared.'

● **LEFT** Alex Cuthbert slices through the Wallaby defence for the Lions' second try, although there was an anxious wait for it to be awarded while the TMO ruled on a possible obstruction.

● **ABOVE** The Wallabies celebrate the award of an 80th-minute penalty against the Lions scrum in Brisbane.
● **FACING PAGE** Kurtley Beale slips on the turf as he takes the potentially match-winning kick, the ball dropping short and wide.

That criticism stung. In the immediate aftermath, the Wallabies were more concerned in doing a head count on their wounded. There was some consolation to be had in defeat, notably the electrifying debut of Folau. 'Izzy is not intimidated and he's quick,' said Robbie Deans. 'When you've got that sort of capacity to play, it tends to slow the game down, slows the defence down because they're conscious of all his options and he's very good at taking those options. He's a talent and we need to bring him into the game.'

That was a veiled criticism of his own fly half, who just did not manage to work Folau into the game enough in the second half. What might have been, eh?

Instead it was the Lions who wore the smiles. Captain Sam Warburton, who had seen so many games against Australia over the last 12 months slip away at the death, admitted that it had been 'the longest minute of my life', as Beale lined up the kick for goal.

Celebrations in the Lions dressing room were muted. They knew that they ought to have had it wrapped up earlier.

'It was frantic, tough to control at times, and luckily we have a lot of good leaders in the team that meant we were able to manage the game well at times,' said fly half Jonny Sexton. 'At times we didn't manage it so well. So there are things we need to improve on, and we know there are fine margins and we need to make sure we improve again next week.'

There had been enough drama that night to last an entire series. There was more to come. Overnight, the Wallaby captain, lock forward James Horwill,

was cited for an alleged stamp on the head of his opposite number, Alun Wyn Jones. The hearing was held on the Sunday. The video footage did not look good for Horwill. It showed clear contact. The Wallabies had left Brisbane early that Sunday morning and flown to Melbourne. The Horwill case looked straightforward. After a four-hour hearing it looked less so.

The Wallabies received a timely boost to their cause with news that Horwill had been cleared. The verdict left the Lions gobsmacked. The low-end tariff for such an offence is two weeks, which would have put the highly regarded Wallaby captain out of the

series. The hearing ruled in his favour that the contact had not been intentional. Horwill's defence was that he had been 'off-balance' and had spun into the prostrate Jones.

'After hearing all the evidence I could not find that when Horwill's right foot came into glancing contact with Wyn Jones's face, that Horwill was acting recklessly,' said IRB Judicial Officer Nigel Hampton QC. 'I found that I could not reject as being implausible or improbable Horwill's explanation that as he was driving forward with his right leg raised he was spun off-balance through the impact of the Lions players entering the ruck from the opposite side.

Horwill was understandably relieved.

'Obviously it's never nice hearing stuff like that, but I'm very happy with the process and the result,' said Horwill. 'I'm very relieved. Hopefully I can get some sleep and hit the ground running at training in Melbourne on Monday.'

Gatland had signalled his viewpoint earlier in the day. 'I played in the days when rucking was allowed and I've still got some scars that bear witness to the ruckings I had, but for me the head was sacrosanct and you stayed away from that,' said Gatland.

And so the Horwill case was added to a litany of episodes in the southern hemisphere that had left a sour taste: the Schalk Burger alleged gouging in 2009, the Tana Umaga tackle on Brian O'Driscoll in New Zealand four years earlier, the taking-out of Richard Hill by Nathan Grey in Australia in 2001. It is not just on the pitch that the Lions have had to take on their adversaries.

There was a more considerable dent to their morale to come, with news that Paul O'Connell had fractured his forearm. Horwill reprieved; O'Connell out. The scales of justice did not seem balanced.

The Lions ought to have been in upbeat mood. Instead, as they headed to Melbourne, set back on their heels by this double whammy of disappointing tidings, the momentum seemed to have edged back to the Wallabies. It was going to be an edgy and interesting week.

● RIGHT **The Lions applaud Wallaby skipper James Horwill from the field after the first Test. Horwill was later to be cited for allegedly stamping on Lions lock Alun Wyn Jones.**

■ MATCH 6: Brumbies 14 Lions 12, Canberra, 18 June

WARREN GATLAND

The head coach had this to say after the first Lions defeat to an Australian provincial side since 1971:

■ 'We were building along nicely and everything was going swimmingly – and then you've taken a bit of a knock, but sometimes a reality check is not the worst thing. You just get on the horse again.'

RORY BEST

The Lions hooker and captain for the day knew where it had gone wrong:

■ 'At the breakdown they smashed us.'

GEOFF PARLING

Substitute lock Geoff Parling had a novel take on defeat:

■ 'One of their guys said to me "I could retire now". He said it's the biggest game he's ever going to play.'

■ MATCH 7: FIRST TEST Australlia 21 Lions 23, Brisbane, 22 June

WARREN GATLAND

The head coach gave his thoughts on the match and the result:

■ 'It just shows how close this series is going to be. We saw some great tries. We're pretty happy, although it could have gone either way. But we'll take that and I think we deserved to win.

'What matters is the result. Key factors were the goal-kicking of Leigh Halfpenny and, obviously, the George North try. And there was a fantastic one from Alex Cuthbert.

'The scrum was a bit disappointing in the second half and we probably played a bit too much rugby in our own half in the first period. It wasn't the greatest Test in the world but we've won.'

SAM WARBURTON

The open-side and Lions captain reflected:

■ 'I'm absolutely delighted – it's a great start. But it's only half the job. We celebrated for a bit and then realised that we have to back it up again next week.

'It's great for momentum that we have got the first game sorted. It was entertaining, that's for sure. It was too close for comfort and the last 20 minutes were really hard. You have to give it to Australia. They went all the way.

'The sides are even and that showed as it went down to the last ten seconds. They came out very well in the first 20 minutes, but we weathered the storm and put points on the board.

'When it is taken out of your control with a kick, all you can do is watch. I thought it was going to go over …

'The fans have been immense. From a player's point of view, it doesn't half pick you up when you are tired and blowing in the game. When they suddenly find a voice and get behind you it is a massive lift.

'In our heart of hearts we know we can play better – we know that wasn't our best performance.'

● **BELOW AND FACING PAGE** Two ends of the spectrum. While a delighted Sam Warburton acknowledges his side's victory, Wallaby coach Robbie Deans can only commiserate with Israel Folau after the closest of finishes.

GEORGE NORTH

The fit-again Lions wing reflected on his score:

■ 'I think it is called panic running. It was just a case of run, run, run and run and hopefully the gaps will open. It is up there with the best tries I have scored and I was pretty chuffed to score in my first Test for the Lions.'

ROBBIE DEANS

The Wallaby coach praised his side's display given their injury handicaps:

■ 'They [the injuries] were very frustrating – so to give themselves a chance of winning the game was a courageous performance.'

KURTLEY BEALE

Substitute Kurtley Beale looked back on that potentially match-winning kick:

■ 'It was just unfortunate that the grass under my feet was a bit loose. A scrum was there earlier and ripped up the dirt. It was a bit of bad luck. You can't have any doubts playing Test rugby. It was my turn and I stepped up.'

WILL GENIA

The Australia scrum half recollected what he said to his team-mate after the failed kick:

■ 'He's really good and I said to him "Mate, I don't want to see you upset and I don't want to see you frown. You were outstanding when you came on." He made an impact. I just hope he is not upset about missing one kick.'

JAMES O'CONNOR

The stand-off revealed that he thought it might be him in Beale's place:

■ 'I did think about taking that final kick, but Kurtley came on and he was playing well. You can't put that defeat just down to him.'

JAMES HORWILL

The Wallaby captain also tried his best to put his team-mate's mind at rest:

■ 'No one's blaming anyone. I said "Don't worry about it. These things happen and you have just got to get on with it. Everyone in the team still loves you."'

C/M/S

Allow us to give you
an initial impression of
who we are.

Stand for more.
If CMS isn't a name that you're familiar
with, it's time we brought you up to speed. Put simply, we're the leading
European organisation of law firms with more offices in Europe than any
of our competitors. We pride ourselves on taking a genuine, client-focused
approach to what we do – a style that has seen us work successfully with
some of the world's biggest organisations. And, perhaps most importantly
for those of you looking for a graduate training contract, we can offer you
exposure to multi-jurisdictional work and a guaranteed secondment
opportunity, plus the support and encouragement you need to lay
foundations for a lasting career.

Discover exactly how much more CMS stands for by visiting
www.cms-cmck.com/graduates

Second Test

Changes. Damned if you do. Damned if you don't. The outcome justifies everything. As Warren Gatland said: 'I don't know where this thing about not changing a winning team comes from. You pick a team to get the job done. It's as simple as that.' The Lions management had another audition to sit through before making their call on their line-up for the second Test – the last midweek fixture of the trip, against the Rebels in Melbourne.

● ABOVE **Killer blow. Adam Ashley-Cooper celebrates his 75th-minute try at the Etihad Stadium. Converted by Christian Leali'ifano, it gave Australia victory in the second Test.**

The Lions flew in from Brisbane on the Monday, still digesting the injury and citing news. Teams always put a brave face on it with any setback. They have no option. They would fold pretty quickly if there was not a genuine conviction about making the best of the situation and moving on. Graham Rowntree had mentioned it several times already, this absolute need to 'make [it] up on the hoof'. There are plans and there is the reality of swiftly changing scenarios.

Injury is a stalking horse, ready to mess with the best-laid plans. If there was one man that the Lions did not want to lose it was Paul O'Connell. He was a big figure in the set-up, literally as well as spiritually so. He was a huge presence on the field, a physical power but also a man with an acute rugby brain, aware of all possibilities even when his head was buried deep in a maul. O'Connell was also in prime condition, the legacy of a season spent mainly on the sidelines recuperating from a back injury. He was fierce and unrelenting out on the field, playing as well as he had ever done in his career.

'He is one of the best, and he's in the form of his life as well,' said Rowntree. 'He came into selection quite late because he had been out for so long with injuries during the season. Suddenly, he came back on the radar after that game [for Munster] against Harlequins in the European Cup. He was fit. In fact, I don't think he's ever been fitter. I would like him to stay on tour because of the influence he has around the group. Losing someone like Paul galvanises a squad like us. We are a very tight group.'

More than a mere player, O'Connell was also a totem for many, especially the younger squad

● ABOVE Paul O'Connell considers victory at the end of the first Test in Brisbane. However, a fracture of the right arm suffered in the match put paid to his tour, as a player at least.

● FACING PAGE Quite a week! Geoff Parling became a father, was chosen to captain the midweek Lions, then was selected as a starter for the Melbourne Test. In the event he was rested against the Melbourne Rebels, Dan Lydiate captaining the dirt-trackers.

members. They saw him as a father figure, a rallying point in times of trouble. Fit, fresh and on top of his game – yes, O'Connell's loss would be felt keenly.

The mood was the exact opposite down along Melbourne's famous Collins Street, where the

Wallabies were billeted in a stylish converted city jail. That is where many thought Horwill should be residing, metaphorically speaking, in rugby clink, banged up for his misdeeds. The Horwill case was to become a long-running saga, dragged out to ridiculous lengths. What was not in doubt was the importance of the player to the side, as seminal an influence as O'Connell himself. In fact, probably more so. The Lions did have strength in depth, even if they could not match the calibre of O'Connell's contribution. The Wallabies did not. Horwill was nigh on indispensable. True, they had survived a long stint without him the previous year, but only just. They were monstered 33-6 by France in Paris without him, though they rallied well after that embarrassment. But Horwill was free to play on, for the moment at any rate, the four-hour disciplinary hearing ruling that it could find no compelling evidence to confirm that Horwill had intended to deliberately trample on Alun Wyn Jones. Nigel Hampton QC was one of the few people in the country who saw it that way.

The Lions had to keep their counsel. Privately, they were seething. Publicly, they abided by due process. 'It's happened, we move on,' Rowntree said. 'We have enough to get on with with the Test coming up on Saturday and we accept that decision and get on with it.'

The Lions forwards coach was aware at that time that his principal loose-head prop, Alex Corbisiero, was struggling with a calf injury. At a stroke, two of the Lions' best forwards from the first Test were crook. Yes, Rowntree did have enough to be worrying about.

O'Connell's injury resulted in a reshuffle to the 23 selected for the game against the Melbourne Rebels. It was clear how the Lions were thinking for the Test when Geoff Parling was removed from the line-up entirely. He had been due to captain the Lions, an honour about which he spoke with great pride that Sunday, almost matching the delight with which he had spoken about the birth of his daughter, May Rose, three days earlier. Parling had been linked up with Skype, only for the midwife to do the decent thing and leave him twiddling his thumbs in time-honoured fashion 12,000 miles away. 'Geoff is more than just a line-out forward,' said Rowntree. 'He's a very clever footballer, a good ball carrier, his work-rate involvement is very high and he is getting better and better, but he has got to in a squad like this one.'

Dan Lydiate took over the captaincy for the game against the Rebels, with Ian Evans taking Parling's place in the second row and Tom Croft being drafted on to the replacements' bench.

There was an edge in the air that Tuesday as the Lions took the field against the Rebels at AAMI Park, part of a magnificent sporting complex just a ten-minute walk from the city centre, housing rugby, Rules and tennis. It puts to shame facilities in the

UK. The apprehension was due to a couple of factors. There were Test places up for grabs, with the locks and the back-row boys all looking to impress. Manu Tuilagi was also back in harness after recovering from a shoulder 'stinger' problem suffered a fortnight earlier. A powerful performance from him could see him force his way on to the bench.

Lodged in the consciousness also was that hangdog showing against the Brumbies the previous week. It had been an abject display, one that undermined the ethos of this group who had pledged to honour the badge in every minute of every game. What they lacked in Canberra, they brought to the table in Melbourne as the Lions raced to a 35-0 victory, a win that was as commanding as the scoreline suggests. It was an impressive performance and just the tonic everyone needed.

Flanker Sean O'Brien, scrum half Conor Murray, his replacement Ben Youngs and wing Sean Maitland all scored tries, while there was a second-half penalty try that underlined the Lions' forward dominance. Fly half Owen Farrell kicked three conversions, and Stuart Hogg landed two as they kept the Rebels scoreless. Both O'Brien and Lydiate showed well, their forceful running and gritty tackling serving the Lions well on the night. Tuilagi did as Tuilagi does and made himself a handful. His key asset is obvious – he gets across the gain line – but, for an opposition, knowing that and being able to do something about it are two entirely different things.

'The shoulder felt really good,' said Tuilagi. 'There are no issues. I was straight into it with the contact. I felt good. I just wanted the game to go on. I think a lot of us felt it was the last chance for all the lads that didn't play last Saturday to hold their hands up and do their best for the coaches. We left everything out there, and at the end of the day that is all you can ask or hope for. I feel as though I am back to where I was before the injury.'

Both locks, Richie Gray and Ian Evans, could feel satisfied with their performance. Certainly Evans had been muted on the tour, a surprise given that he

● **LEFT** Sean Maitland bursts for the line during the Lions' 35-0 win over the Melbourne Rebels. The Scotland wing then offloaded inside to Toby Faletau before cropping up later in the move to score in the corner.

had been such an important figure in Wales's Six Nations Championship side.

The Lions were eager to make amends for their only tour defeat seven days earlier, and they started brightly despite losing two early line outs. The Lions' early pressure had to tell and they claimed an opening try after 15 minutes. They drove for the line from a five-metre scrum, and although they were initially thwarted, possession spun backwards and scrum half Conor Murray reacted quickly to pick up and dive over. Farrell converted from the touch line, and he then sacrificed two kickable penalties as the Lions looked to maintain a foothold inside the Rebels 22.

The Lions' second try was one of the best they had constructed all tour. Tuilagi made it possible through a barnstorming run just inside the Rebels half and his brilliant offload freed Maitland who then found Faletau, but the Wales No. 8 was denied a try when he slipped. The tourists quickly recycled possession via Brad Barritt and Simon Zebo, which enabled Maitland to touch down for a try that Farrell again converted.

The Lions were determined to go through their repertoire, turning down kicks at goal so that they could polish their moves. Early in the second half Farrell again kicked to the corner as the Lions went for a line-out option, and such boldness reaped its reward as Faletau found skipper Dan Lydiate, who delivered the final pass to O'Brien.

Farrell maintained his accuracy from the touch line as his third successful conversion made it 21-0. He was then replaced by Hogg as Gatland cast an eye towards Saturday's Test.

Further changes followed five minutes later, with four forwards joining the action, including Lions debutant Tom Court, who had only linked up with the squad the previous day. The penalty try came 16 minutes from time, when Rebels forward Jordy Reid illegally halted a Lions attack, and as he made his way to the sin-bin, Hogg converted. The Lions had enough time to unlock their opponents one more time, when Ben Youngs claimed a superb solo effort

● RIGHT **Melbourne Rebels stand-off Bryce Hegarty feels the double impact of opposite number Owen Farrell and Lions captain for the day Dan Lydiate.**

after he broke clear from a line out just outside the Rebels 22. Hogg converted and it was job done for the Lions.

'That was a good response to the disappointment of last week,' said Gatland. 'The spirit really came out today, demonstrated by the way we didn't concede any points. There's still an opportunity for people to be involved because there are two games. Given the attrition rate, there are bound to be a few injuries between now and the final Test.'

For the Melbourne Test, Gatland was true to his word about picking a side that he felt could get a job done regardless of the fact that the first Test had been won. There were five changes to the XV that had started in Brisbane, a sure sign that the management felt that the Lions could improve. Two of the changes were enforced, with Mako Vunipola stepping up from the bench and, as signposted,

Geoff Parling being handed the tricky task of filling the O'Connell shoes. Big shoes, big task.

There was good news in the return of Tommy Bowe to the colours, completing a remarkable recovery from the broken hand he sustained on the opening weekend in Australia. Bowe was to wear a hurling glove to protect his hand. Alex Cuthbert was the unlucky one to make way for Bowe, even though the young Welshman had scored such a stunning try at the Suncorp. Gatland, though, was a huge fan of Bowe, understandably so given that he had seen him at close quarters on the 2009 tour.

There was a surprise at scrum half, where Mike Phillips was overlooked in favour of Ben Youngs. The reasoning behind the change was curious. Gatland insisted that Phillips was 'fit', only to then point out that he had been tending to his sore knee and had not been able to train fully. Gatland said that they

wanted to hold him back for the third Test. It didn't make much sense, much as Youngs deserved a crack. His form had been pretty perky on tour, a poor evening against the Brumbies apart.

The other starting change saw Lydiate brought on to the flank in place of Tom Croft. The Lions figured that they had line-out prowess through Parling and wanted Lydiate's chop-chop style in the tackle to tame Will Genia. Gatland stockpiled his bench with back-rowers as O'Brien and Croft were both given the nod. It left the Lions at risk if there were to be an injury at lock, as there was no specialist cover.

Gatland knew exactly how intense Saturday night was going to be. 'This is a do-or-die match for Australia,' said Gatland. 'It is going to be a real battle out there. We have decided to add a bit more physicality to our side up front. We have chosen

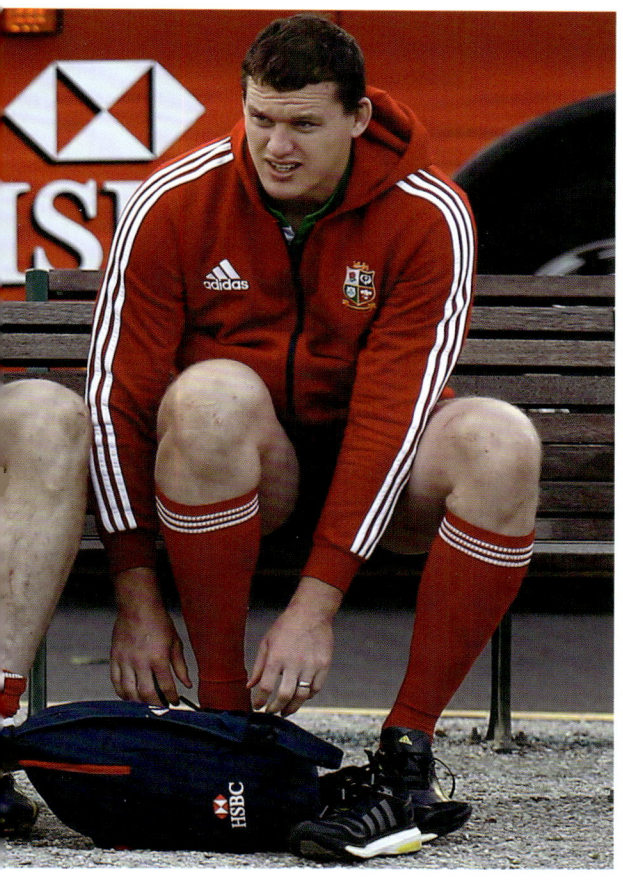

● ABOVE Joe Tomane was given the Wallaby No. 11 shirt for the Melbourne game, replacing Digby Ioane.
● LEFT Richard Hibbard, fit-again Tommy Bowe and the giant lock forwards Richie Gray and Ian Evans prepare for a training session in Melbourne a couple of days before the second Test.
● PAGES 96-97 Another scrum disintegrates during the second Test. The Lions were under the pump at scrum time early in the game but eventually gained the upper hand.

horses for courses. Australia are going to be absolutely desperate for this. As it was four years ago in South Africa, this is going to be brutal. They are going to throw the kitchen sink at us. It is all-or-nothing for them. We have to handle that. We can win this series by winning on Saturday and that's where our whole focus needs to be. The last thing we want to think about is it being one all and having to play another game in Sydney. It is all about Saturday night.'

Australia had regrouped well from their own troubles and were able to name a side that actually looked stronger than the one that had suffered all those injury blows the previous week. Surprisingly,

● BELOW No way out. Lions scrum half Ben Youngs finds himself encircled by Wallabies at the Etihad Stadium.
● FACING PAGE Ben Mowen lines up Brian O'Driscoll as the Lions centre reaches for an awkward ball during the second Test.
● PAGES 100-101 Alun Wyn Jones of the Lions stretches in vain as the ball sails towards the waiting hands of Wallaby back-rower Ben Mowen.

Christian Leali'ifano was passed fit to play despite having been knocked cold in the opening minute in Brisbane. His availability was crucial for the Wallabies, as a second playmaker and as a goal-kicker.

Australia had had a curious week, first with a warrant issued for the arrest of wing Digby Ioane for a missed court appearance and then with late-night shenanigans involving Kurtley Beale and James O'Connor. Joe Tomane was drafted on the wing, with Beale taking the place of the injured Berrick Barnes at full back.

The mood had shifted from the previous week, when there was romance in the air, lots of froth about the fans and the noise and the colour. Now it was about glory or survival. The backdrop was just that – a backdrop. There was a ground record crowd (56,771) for a sporting event packed into the Etihad Stadium, the Colonial as it once was, the scene of Lions heartache before in 2001, when the second Test was lost in spectacular fashion after the Lions had appeared to be cruising.

There was to be no meltdown this time from the Lions, but there was to be the same grief. Just as Australia would not have deserved victory in the first Test if Kurtley had struck gold rather than slipped like a park footballer, so too the Lions would not have deserved to be whooping and hollering if Leigh Halfpenny's last-gasp effort from 55 metres had gone over. Mind you, they wouldn't have cared too much about just deserts.

The Lions had been leading from around the half-hour mark, easing out to 15-9 thanks to the boot of Halfpenny, and with five minutes remaining, still held that advantage. It was not easy figuring out how they held sway. They had suffered in the scrummage, particularly in the early stages. Prop Mako Vunipola fell foul of referee Craig Joubert, giving away three penalties. More even than that, the Wallabies began to feel good about themselves. Were they not supposed to be rolled over by the northern brutes, a soft touch in the scrum and lacking poundage out where it mattered?

● **BELOW** Need a lift? George North picks up opposite number Israel Folau, who had tried to tackle the Lions wing, and takes him with him as he moves upfield, much to the crowd's delight.
● **FACING PAGE** Skipper Sam Warburton is helped from the Etihad turf by the Lions medical team after damaging a hamstring in the final quarter of the match.

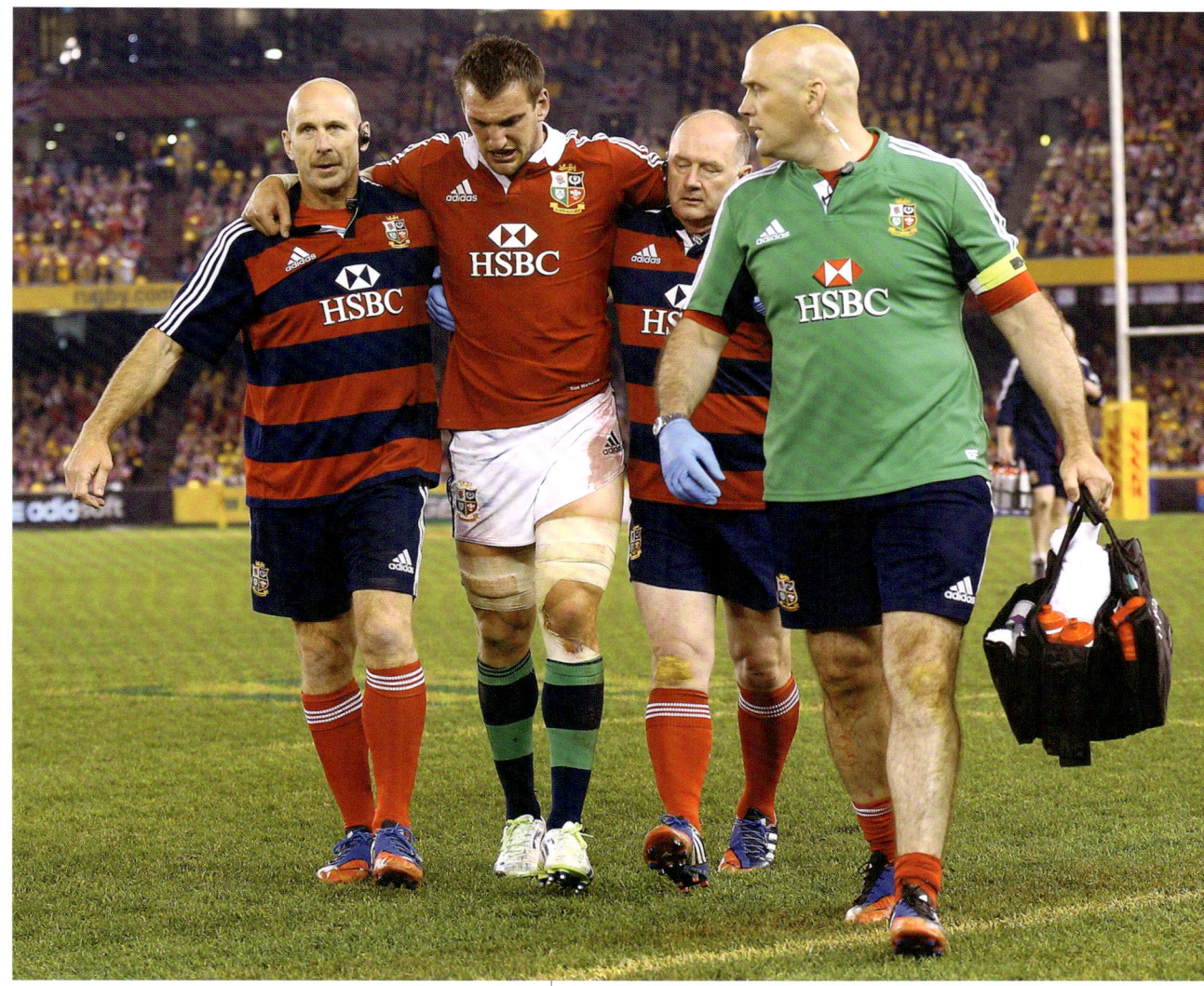

There was no sign of that in Melbourne. In fact, in those opening exchanges, the Wallabies were so assured that they even opted for scrums. Somewhere deep in the south of France where he is now based, Andrew Sheridan, the scourge of the Wallabies on a couple of occasions, would have watched with bemusement. Wouldn't have happened in his day.

The Lions did manage to rouse themselves and actually became dominant in the scrum the longer the game wore on. Once again, the complex absurdity that is the modern scrum, where so few have a clue as to what is going on, including the officials, came into play. Vunipola looked as if he was about to be substituted at any time during that torrid spell. As it was, he lasted the distance, the full 80 minutes, a rare feat for any prop these days. Curious.

There was little stability about the Lions set-piece play. Their line out never managed to plant its feet on the Etihad turf and set the foundations on which the back line could play. By comparison with the blistering first Test, there was far less fluency and bite in the play of either side. There were four cracking tries in Brisbane. There was one here, a workmanlike, well-taken effort by Adam Ashley-Cooper in the 75th minute.

But the match was never less than compelling. There were numerous handling errors, lots of kicking, not much of it pinpoint accurate or accompanied by a thundering chase, and plenty of parry and thrust. It was impossible to take your eyes away from the action, fractured as it was.

There was a pervasive air of tension from first whistle to last. The exchanges were nip and tuck, with the kickers trading blows. Australia had Leali'ifano in the ranks for this Test and it made all the difference. No wonder they got the wet sponge on to him quickly the previous week when he had been knocked out. He didn't miss a thing all night.

The same is usually written about Halfpenny. Here he had two blemishes, the first an early effort which looked on the mark, only to drop on to the

crossbar. Nevertheless, the Lions had made a lively start, and looked set fair. A ninth-minute Halfpenny strike made it 3-0.

That fault line in the scrum, though, soon told. How the Lions missed the injured Corbisiero. When Vunipola was adjudged to have collapsed a 16th-minute scrum, Leali'ifano stepped up to land an equalising penalty.

Things rapidly deteriorated for the Saracens loose-head when he was whistled again by referee Joubert, and Leali'ifano slotted a second penalty before Halfpenny cancelled out that kick five minutes later. Australia, though, wheeled a scrum and Halfpenny completed his penalty hat-trick.

But Leali'ifano also maintained outstanding accuracy, making it three penalties from three attempts just before half-time, yet there was still time for Halfpenny to restore the Lions' three-point

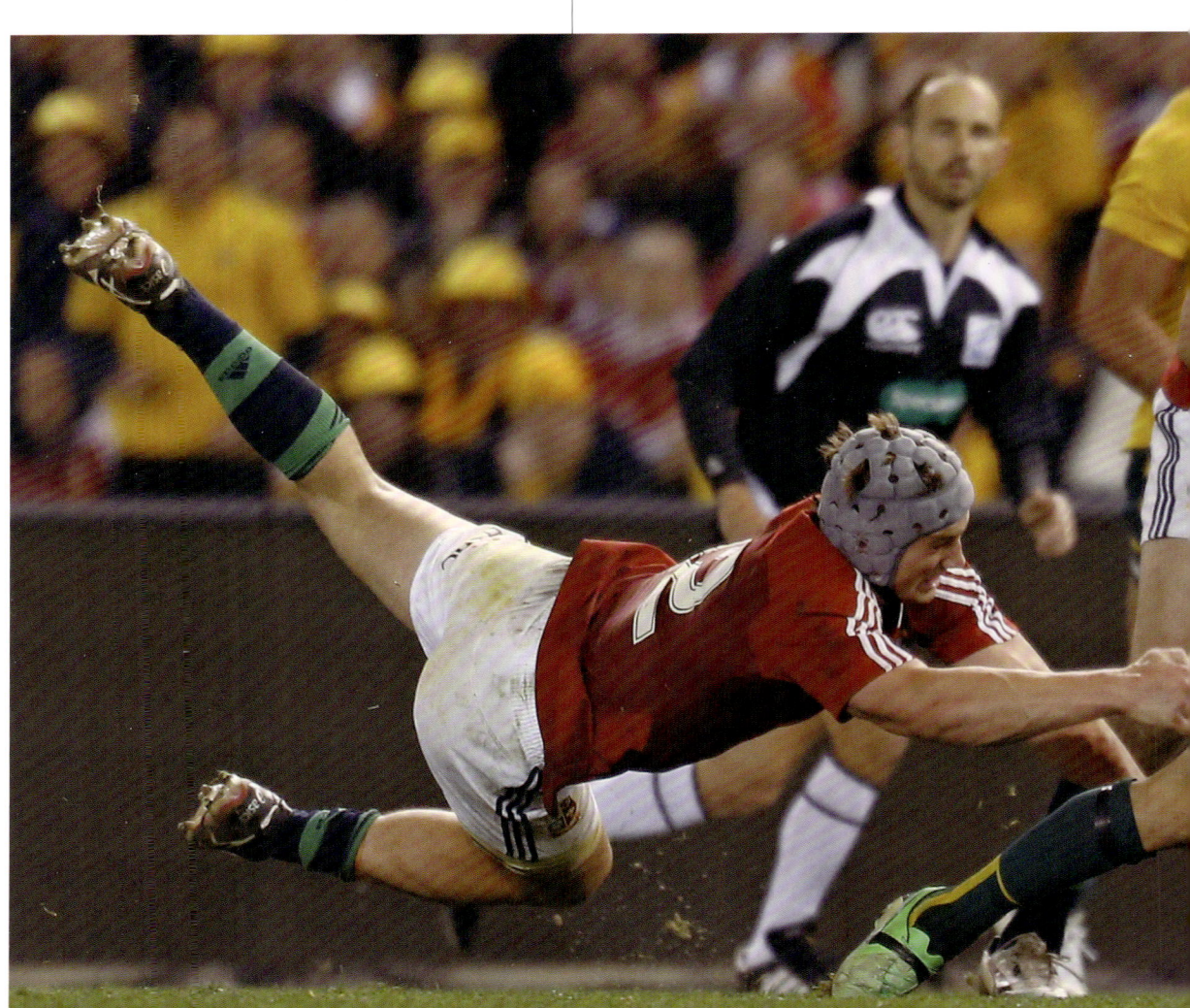

advantage after Joubert punished Wallaby flanker Ben Mowen for not rolling away.

The Lions led 12-9 at the interval, but fortuitously so. They had tried a few things but nothing had come off. At one stage they put 11 players in a line out, yet they lacked a clinical edge and Australia looked the more likely try scorers during an opening 40 minutes high on endeavour and effort but lacking creative brilliance.

The high error count continued early in the second period, with both sides struggling to keep hold of possession. No one was immune from the messy play. Lions centre Brian O'Driscoll threw a wild pass that ended up in the hands of Australia's principal danger man, Israel Folau.

Gatland then made his first change, sending on Conor Murray at scrum half for Ben Youngs after 54 minutes, which was quickly followed by Youngs's brother – hooker Tom – being replaced by Richard Hibbard. A scoreless third quarter meant the Lions maintained their slender lead. Having come down heavily after picking up Folau bodily and carrying

● LEFT Jonathan Davies is powerless to stop Adam Ashley-Cooper as the Wallaby centre crosses from short range to score the only try of the second Test.

● ABOVE Steady nerve. Christian Leali'ifano slots the conversion to put the Wallabies 16-15 up with little time left.

him along on the charge, North quickly returned to action, before Halfpenny rifled over a penalty from halfway. The Lions looked as though they could breathe easily, despite losing Sam Warburton for the final stages, the captain trudging off with a hamstring problem. It didn't look at all good for Warburton's prospects of making the third Test.

There was a gathering sense that Australia were growing stronger. But still the Lions held on grimly. Australia, though, had their dander up. They

stormed deep into the Lions 22, driven forward by hooker Stephen Moore, who had been one of the stand-out performers in the series.

The Lions tackled prodigiously, yet wave after wave of Wallaby attacks had to take a toll, and

Ashley-Cooper smashed through Jonathan Davies for a try that had a certain inevitability about it. Leali'ifano still had a fair bit to do. He was two-thirds of the way out to the touch line, on the left-hand side. His old-fashioned draw style, though, was in perfect working order, the ball setting out towards the right post and curling in beautifully. It was to be the clincher. 16-15 to Australia.

There was one final drama to come, of course, and it centred on the man who had been such a rock for the Lions – Leigh Halfpenny. It was two minutes into added time when the Joubert whistle went again. The entire stadium gasped. The Australian fans, as well as players, looked at the ref in horror. Surely not? But, yes, the arm was raised, and then came the point to the posts. Halfpenny was going to take it on. Of course he was. This was the moment he had been rehearsing since he was a boy being picked up outside school by his grandfather, Malcolm, near the family home in Swansea. Five nights a week, Halfpenny would go through his routines on a field in Gorseinon. He would see the posts, work out the angles, take a deep breath, run up and swing. In his dreams, it would always go over, sail between the posts, and glory would be his.

It was not to be this time. It was a brute of a kick, a long effort, with a bit of angle and in the last minute of a punishing Test. It would have been miraculous if he had managed to nail it. But he didn't. The whistle blew and Halfpenny stood there, transfixed, desolate, alone. Such is the life of a kicker. Cruel, terribly cruel. Halfpenny, who had landed 32 from 35 attempts prior to that, was inconsolable, as Kurtley Beale had been the week before. There really was so little to choose between the sides.

'I obviously hoped that Halfpenny would miss although he's hardly missed a kick all tour so your pulse rate certainly goes up,' said Wallaby captain James Horwill, a man whose delight at the final whistle was tempered by the fact that he faced an appeal hearing on the Monday night. 'We were disappointed to let them have a shot at goal like that. We should have run the clock down and closed

● LEFT We have been here before. Jonny Sexton looks on, while a Wallaby benchman cannot bear to, as Leigh Halfpenny lines up the last-gasp kick to decide the second Test.

the game out with more composure. We found a way to win. It probably wasn't the prettiest game of rugby, but we found a way to win. There's relief and jubilation. These are intense battles that come down to one moment. Now all bets are off. It's one game to win it.'

Robbie Deans could not conceal his own satisfaction, a feeling of vindication perhaps, given that his own future was in the balance. 'I'm very proud,' said Deans. 'It doesn't get any bigger than that. They knew that if they didn't score a try and conversion the series would be done. There's one Test to go. How good is that? What a great series! It's great for the game and Saturday will be a great end to the series.'

● BELOW It's 16-15 to Australia! The final whistle brings elation for Wallaby skipper James Horwill and prop Sekope Kepu.
● FACING PAGE Leigh Halfpenny is alone with his thoughts in the middle of the Etihad Stadium after his long-range penalty attempt for a Lions victory falls short.

Halfpenny had missed only four kicks all tour – completing 32 out of 36 – and Warburton refused to blame his Wales team-mate for an agonising result. 'I've seen Leigh kick those before so it was a good decision to go for the three points. In training he'll bang them over,' Warburton said. 'He just didn't connect on this occasion, but he can't blame himself because it was an extremely difficult kick. Come Monday morning he'll be fine and as good as gold. It was a realistic chance to win the Test series and if I'd still been on the pitch I would have looked at Leigh straightaway and told him to go for it.'

The Lions did not have much time to mull over their thoughts. They were packed and on a plane to Noosa on Queensland's Sunshine Coast early the next morning. It was a pre-planned break, a chance to recharge. They certainly needed to do that. Momentum had shifted. The pendulum had swung Australia's way. The Lions landed and were quickly in the Pacific surf for a recovery session. Waving or drowning? We would soon find out.

OPINION Matches 8−9

■ **MATCH 8:** *Melbourne Rebels 0 Lions 35, Melbourne, 25 June*

WARREN GATLAND

The Lions head coach declared that the management were happy with their side's performance against the Rebels:

■ *'We're really pleased …*

'They were thoroughly professional. For some it might be their last game on tour, so they wanted to finish strongly.

'The message was that there was an opportunity to be in the squad for Saturday. If Beale had got one kick, would we be discussing what changes we would need? So we emphasised to the squad saying "Your tour's not over".'

OWEN FARRELL

The fly half explained that some changes had been made to his game:

■ *'I've been asked to play wider and flatter, which I'm comfortable with. I was trying to make sure we kept going forward and we kept getting quick ball. If it keeps going like this I will be extremely happy by the end of the tour.'*

■ **MATCH 9:** *SECOND TEST Australia 16 Lions 15, Melbourne, 29 June*

SAM WARBURTON

The captain, now doubtful for the third Test, reflected on what had happened:

■ *'We're going through what Australia went through last week. There is still a Test series up for grabs and by no means is this over. We are a very determined bunch of players.*

'Australia got hold of us when they got territory in our 22 and we found it difficult to get out. Territory is everything in games like this.'

WARREN GATLAND

The head coach believed the Lions did not manage the game as well as they might have:

■ *'Test rugby is about game management – managing a couple of crucial line outs or turnovers. Even when they made mistakes and the referee said "advantage over", we didn't make the most of it.*

'We were pretty comfortable at half-time, but, being

● **RIGHT** Having struggled from the tee in Brisbane, the Wallabies did not waste any shots at goal in Melbourne, thanks to restored centre Christian Leali'ifano, who struck four from four.
● **FACING PAGE** Loose-head Mako Vunipola had had a rampaging tour with ball in hand but struggled in the set-piece scrum in Melbourne – at least at first.

Australia, they never give up and keep plugging away. At 15-9 we thought "Keep our head and keep our composure", but they took the opportunities that went their way. We didn't control the territory very well. We weren't smart enough and didn't look after the ball.
'We were disappointed with a few things, including penalties at scrums. But until we get some clarity from referees, you've got to take the good with the bad. It's just the way the scrum is refereed.'

ALUN WYN JONES
The lock spoke from the heart of the action:
■ *'In the scrum we seemed to be on the end of a barrage of penalties. We feel hard done by.'*

TOM YOUNGS
The Lions hooker maintained the theme and indicated that his prop Mako Vunipola was the referee's target:
■ *'Huge decisions did not go our way. Credit to Mako – he stuck with it. You have to talk to Mako and say "Stay with it". We will work on the scrums.'*

BRIAN O'DRISCOLL
The veteran centre had this to say:
■ *'We weren't in control, because six points clear is a horrible margin. They battled away, but we weren't able to put enough phases together. After today the momentum is with them.'*

ANDY FARRELL
The Lions defence coach reflected the day after the Test:
■ *'We were lucky to win the first game, but could have won the second. 1-1 is a fair way to look at it.'*

ADAM ASHLEY-COOPER
The Australian try scorer put forward his view:
■ *'Test football is about grinding it out until the 80th minute. The key messages were about ball possession. We knew points would come through penalties or through space.'*

JAMES HORWILL
Wallaby captain Horwill pointed out the similarities with the previous week:
■ *'When their kick didn't go over it was a turnaround – a replay of last week, but switching sides. The attitude has always been there, but we have struggled to get our rhythm.'*

ROBBIE DEANS
The coach was happy with his charges and singled out the Wallaby goal-kicker for praise:
■ *'We held our composure and the new parts of the group are coming together.*
'Leali'ifano is class. It was remarkable on his debut – because that's what it was. He's clearly got a big future if he can deal with that kind of pressure.'

CHRISTIAN LEALI'IFANO
The goal-kicking centre confessed to a few nerves first up:
■ *'I was nervous after missing one kick in warm-ups. You don't want to read too much into that, so once the first kick went over and the crowd went nuts it was good for my confidence.'*

THE LIONS HAVE BEEN FED

Congratulations to The British & Irish Lions
on their successful Tour of Australia.

ABOVE AND BEYOND

OFFICIAL
GLOBAL
SPONSOR

Third Test

They came to Noosa in search of rest. They created pandemonium. The Lions managed to recharge batteries on the Sunshine Coast. They frolicked in the surf, using the chill waters of the Pacific Ocean to soothe the pain, psychological as well as physical, from the previous day's setback. One of those pictured in the waves was Brian O'Driscoll. Little did he know that the peace of the retreat was to be abruptly broken with a tap on the shoulder by the coffee machine three days later.

Warren Gatland had scheduled this break come what may, series won, lost, or tied as it was now. He figured that the players would need a change of scene and some down time. And he was right. His reasoning was part scientific, part hunch. There is a bit of the Brian Clough in the way Gatland operates, happy to let his charges kick back and have a few drinks. But there is an awful lot of detailed science that goes into it all as well. Gatland was the first coach in the Premiership to tune in to the need for peaking in a season, to hit the play-offs in prime shape. He has made a thing of getting his conditioning spot on. He knew what he was doing.

● **ABOVE** Loose-head prop Alex Corbisiero, restored to the side after succumbing to injury in the first Test in Brisbane, touches down in the second minute to give the Lions a flying start in the decider in Sydney.

The players did as they pleased for two days. There was no rugby, no meetings, no analysis. It was time to clear the head. Gatland copped some criticism for taking the squad away from the Test city, Sydney, but he was right to do so. Of course, it was not without its risks. England had done something similar in the 2011 World Cup in New Zealand, decamping to Queenstown. That had backfired horribly. Gatland knew he could trust his men. Well, with one finger crossed.

The Lions did not exist in a total vacuum. Far from it. There was still a lot going on. Barely a day had passed on the entire trip without some sort of news breaking. That is the nature of the beast – multi-headed. That Monday saw confirmation that Sam Warburton's hamstring was indeed mangled. He was out of the tour and might even miss the start of the following season. It was a bitter blow for Warburton, who was hitting top form after a slow

start. He had little need to vindicate himself to Gatland, who knew his capabilities only too well. But he did need to show the outside world that he was the stand-out open-side flanker in the squad. He did not want to be a token selection just because he had the captain's asterisk alongside his name. He wanted to be considered as a player worthy of his place first and foremost. In Melbourne he had achieved just that, playing with vigour, intelligence and zeal. He would be a loss.

That was another Lions captain down, following the fractured arm sustained by Paul O'Connell in the first Test. Two down, one to go.

There was still a good chance that Australia would lose their leader. The IRB-induced appeal against the original decision to clear James Horwill was heard that Monday night in Sydney. It was a pretty unusual situation, the IRB stepping in because they did not think the original verdict projected an image of the game they supported. Horwill would surely cop a ban this time.

But no. Or eventually no. The Monday session delivered no verdict, the matter deferred while the Canadian independent appeal officer, Graeme Mew – hooked up by conference call to Horwill – deliberated. And the Aussie contingent went to bed. News that the original decision had been upheld did not come until Tuesday morning. Horwill was free to play – again. Given his visible emotional response at the final whistle in Melbourne, you might have imagined that he felt it had been his last shot at the Lions. He was reprieved. And happy.

'I'm very relieved,' said Horwill. 'The two hearings have been very fair. I was confident because I knew what happened and I'm glad the right result was made in the end. I love what I do and it means a hell of a lot to me to lead my country in what is probably the biggest game since the World Cup final in 2003. I feel vindicated by the ruling.'

● LEFT A pensive-looking James Horwill at a Wallaby recovery session at Coogee Beach, Sydney, the Monday after the second Test. The IRB's appeal against the decision to clear Horwill of an alleged stamp on Alun Wyn Jones was to be heard that night.
● FACING PAGE Brian O'Driscoll attends training at Noosa, Queensland, on Wednesday 3 July, the day he learned he had been left out of the Lions 23 for the third Test.

● ABOVE The Lions skipper for the third Test, Alun Wyn Jones, trains ahead of the match with recovered centre Jamie Roberts, who would line up alongside Jonathan Davies in Sydney.
● FACING PAGE Warren Gatland, pictured here with Rob Howley, drew a lot of flak over his decision to omit Brian O'Driscoll but believed he had made 'the right rugby decision'.

Mew's reasoning was that all proper procedure had been followed.

'There was sufficient evidence upon which a reasonable judicial officer could have reached the decision that was made,' Mew said. 'Accordingly it could not be said that the judicial officer was manifestly wrong or that the interests of justice otherwise required his decision be overturned. For the appeal to succeed the IRB would have to establish that there was some misapprehension of law or principle by the judicial officer or that his decision was so clearly wrong or manifestly unreasonable that no judicial officer could have reached the conclusion that he did.'

There you have it – complex legalese. Several hundred miles to the north, a much simpler statement was to shatter the tranquillity of an out-of-season resort.

Gatland met with his coaches on Tuesday night. The gathering lasted an hour. It was 'lively', according to Gatland. The head coach is a man who knows his own mind. Once it is made up, he sticks by it. Even so, the decision to leave out O'Driscoll would have involved a good bit of soul-searching. Gatland was later to argue that in the end it came down to rugby logic and once he had decided that he preferred going with the all-Wales pairing of Jamie Roberts and Jonathan Davies, for the attraction of their ingrained familiarity and the benefit of Davies' left boot, he was not for turning.

It was the single most momentous selection decision in recent Lions history and possibly ever. O'Driscoll had never been dropped in his professional career. He had played 133 Tests for Ireland and the Lions. He had captained the Lions in 2005, a tour of duty that had ended with the trauma of being tip-tackled on his neck by Tana Umaga and

● ABOVE Problems for Ben Alexander in the scrum as the Lions impose themselves in Sydney. The Wallaby prop was yellow-carded and replaced immediately his spell in the sin-bin expired.
● FACING PAGE Israel Folau, who was himself soon to depart with a hamstring injury, looks on as a decidedly groggy George Smith is led from the field after a fearsome clash of heads with Richard Hibbard. The veteran Smith later returned to the fray.

Keven Mealamu. He had made his Lions debut in 2001 in Brisbane, scoring a magical try in that night of glory at the Gabba. He had been on four tours but had not featured in a winning Lions series.

This was supposed to be his moment. There was little to choose between him and Davies as outside centres. You could make a case for either player, each with their strengths, each with their weaker points. O'Driscoll was fierce at the breakdown; Davies offered a better kicking option. You could go on endlessly, totting up respective virtues to prove your point.

What brooked no argument was that O'Driscoll was the vastly more experienced leader. At the very moment that the Wallabies were about to reach back into the past to recall veteran flanker George Smith, the Lions decided that experience alone did not provide an overriding reason to select a player. Gatland was asked if he thought captaincy was overrated. 'Yes' was his reply.

There were six changes to the starting line-up. Only one drew fierce critical fire.

'It's only hard because you are making the decision by using your head and not your heart,' said Gatland. 'Then you realise that what comes of making a decision like that is all the peripheral stuff – not the rugby decision – because it becomes a major story for 48 hours and it becomes a debate.

That is the process I've gone through myself. If I go back to the UK after this and say "Did I make the decision because I believe it's the right decision?" or "Did I make the decision because it was the right political decision or a sentimental one?" I have to put [my] hand on my heart and say it's the right rugby decision. I would hate to think we had made calls on trying to avoid criticism or public favour. Sometimes it happens and we've made a really tough decision, a tough call and that's part of it. Brian has been around for a long time. He understands how things work. He is a professional and he appreciated

the fact we had the conversation with him. It's not everyone we always speak to, but he was one that definitely needed the respect of being spoken to.'

Gatland knew that there would be a reaction to his selection. He didn't anticipate quite how ferocious it would be. He was assailed from all sides. Keith Wood weighed in, suggesting that Gatland did not wholly empathise with the concept of the Lions. Another former Irish Lion, Willie John McBride, was also strident in his denunciation. There was even a reaction from Northern Ireland deputy First Minister Martin McGuinness, who thought the decision 'mind-boggling'.

There was more and there was worse. It was only after victory had been secured at the ANZ Stadium that Gatland revealed just how much he had been affected by what he called the 'vitriolic' abuse. It was not an easy few days.

There was another factor at work. There were ten Welshmen named in the starting line-up, more than Wales had ever managed during the golden era of the 1970s and their largest contribution since 1950. Mind you, there had been 11 Englishmen named in 1993 and there had been no outcry. There was this time, a pitiful reaction. These were Lions, not Welsh or English or Irish. And, yes, there was a Scot, Richie Gray, deservedly forcing his way on to the bench.

The return of Roberts was a boost. His power on the cutback run had been missed. Alex Corbisiero was also a welcome addition. The scrum had not been anything like as assured in his absence in Melbourne.

It was not difficult to detect the tone of the selections – power was the name of the game. Richard Hibbard got the nod at hooker over Tom Youngs as the Lions beefed up the scrum, with Sean O'Brien stepping up for Warburton. Toby Faletau was the preferred option at No. 8. Mike Phillips was also back in harness at scrum half.

Alun Wyn Jones was to be captain. He had only captained Wales once. Gatland had looked to four others before him in Wales when naming a captain. 'We picked what we think is the best team,' Gatland added. 'We decided who we feel will do the best job as captain afterwards.'

● RIGHT **A sensational tap-tackle by lock Geoff Parling fells Jesse Mogg as he rockets upfield. The Brumbies speedster had replaced the injured Israel Folau after 27 minutes.**
● PAGES 122-123 **Sean O'Brien, in for the injured Sam Warburton, clatters Wallaby captain James Horwill into touch.**

Roberts was delighted that he had made the cut. There was a shot of him trudging down the tunnel after he injured his hamstring against the Waratahs, shoulders hunched, convinced his tour was over. But it wasn't. Once again, the medics worked wonders. Roberts grafted his way back to fitness, even managing to take time out to do a stint with his rock heroes, the Manic Street Preachers, in Melbourne.

'That was a good experience,' said Roberts. 'I adored the Manics growing up. I am that sort of guy in life who takes every opportunity that comes their way. You just have to get completely excited about this match, not shy away from it, not get nervous. It's just pure excitement, go out and express yourself, keep your concentration and deliver under pressure. I see it as a responsibility. I've been picked to do a job and it is important I deliver. I've always thought that I thrive under pressure in big games, it's where I like to play. I see myself as one of those guys who has to lead the way.'

Only six players – Davies, full back Leigh Halfpenny, wing George North, fly half Jonathan Sexton, prop Adam Jones and lock Alun Wyn Jones – were to head home having started all three Tests.

Change, though, was to prove stimulating rather than unsettling. There was a wholly different air about this Lions side. And it showed immediately at the ANZ Stadium that Saturday night. Once again, the scene was colourful and raucous. There was an extra frisson. The series was on the line. This was the culmination of six weeks of playing, 12 months and more of planning.

And it was to go the Lions' way. It helps, of course, when Will Genia fumbles the kick-off. Genia – the heartbeat of the Wallaby side, a player who, time and again, had been the prompt for an Australian attack, seeing possibilities where others saw difficulty. He who could do no wrong, did wrong.

It got the Lions off to the start they craved. Never might they have imagined that they would get off to such a flyer. From that knock-on, they struck. Corbisiero got an early shunt in the scrum and the Lions pressed, sending Tommy Bowe at the line. The Wallabies were under the cosh already and the Lions piled in to take full advantage, Corbisiero burrowing through for a try after 80 seconds. Wow! That sent the decibel count soaring. Halfpenny converted and then added a penalty from 50 metres, a carbon copy of his last effort in Melbourne, apart from the minor matter that this one soared through the posts, banishing the demons of the previous week.

● LEFT Mike Phillips cannot stop James O'Connor from touching down for Australia bang on half-time. The fly half had jinked his way to the line through a seemingly impenetrable wall of Lions.

121

● ABOVE **57th minute.** The blitz starts here. Jonny Sexton is about to touch down for the first of three second-half Lions tries that sent the Wallaby fightback into reverse.

● FACING PAGE **65th minute.** Leigh Halfpenny steps Will Genia and Joe Tomane and sets off upfield before handing on to George North tearing up on the outside.

● RIGHT George North takes Halfpenny's pass and heads for home, cheered all the way by euphoric Lions fans.

The Lions were rampant. Everything went their way, while Australia toiled and suffered. George Smith got knocked senseless in a collision with Richard Hibbard, leaving the field looking decidedly groggy, only to return. That seemed unwise.

It was to get worse, even if Christian Leali'ifano did manage to bang over a penalty goal. The Wallaby scrum was in terrible straits. Corbisiero was doing a job on his opposite number, Ben Alexander, aided by the power and technique of his front-row muckers, Hibbard and Adam Jones. French referee Romain Poite, renowned for his understanding of the set-piece, knew where the fault lay. He was warning Horwill within 15 minutes that he would have no option but to get heavy if the Wallabies did not sort out their scrum.

They didn't. And Poite was as good as his word, reaching in to brandish yellow to Alexander in the

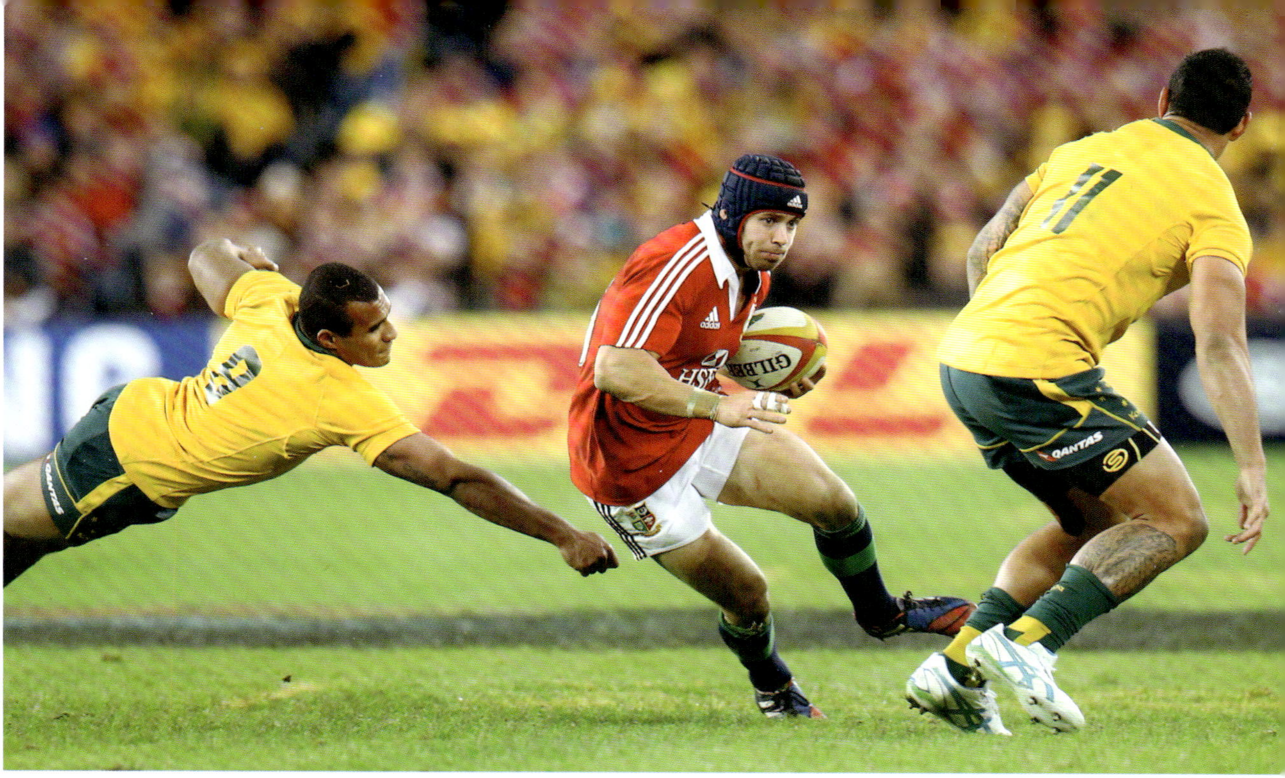
DHL
QANTAS

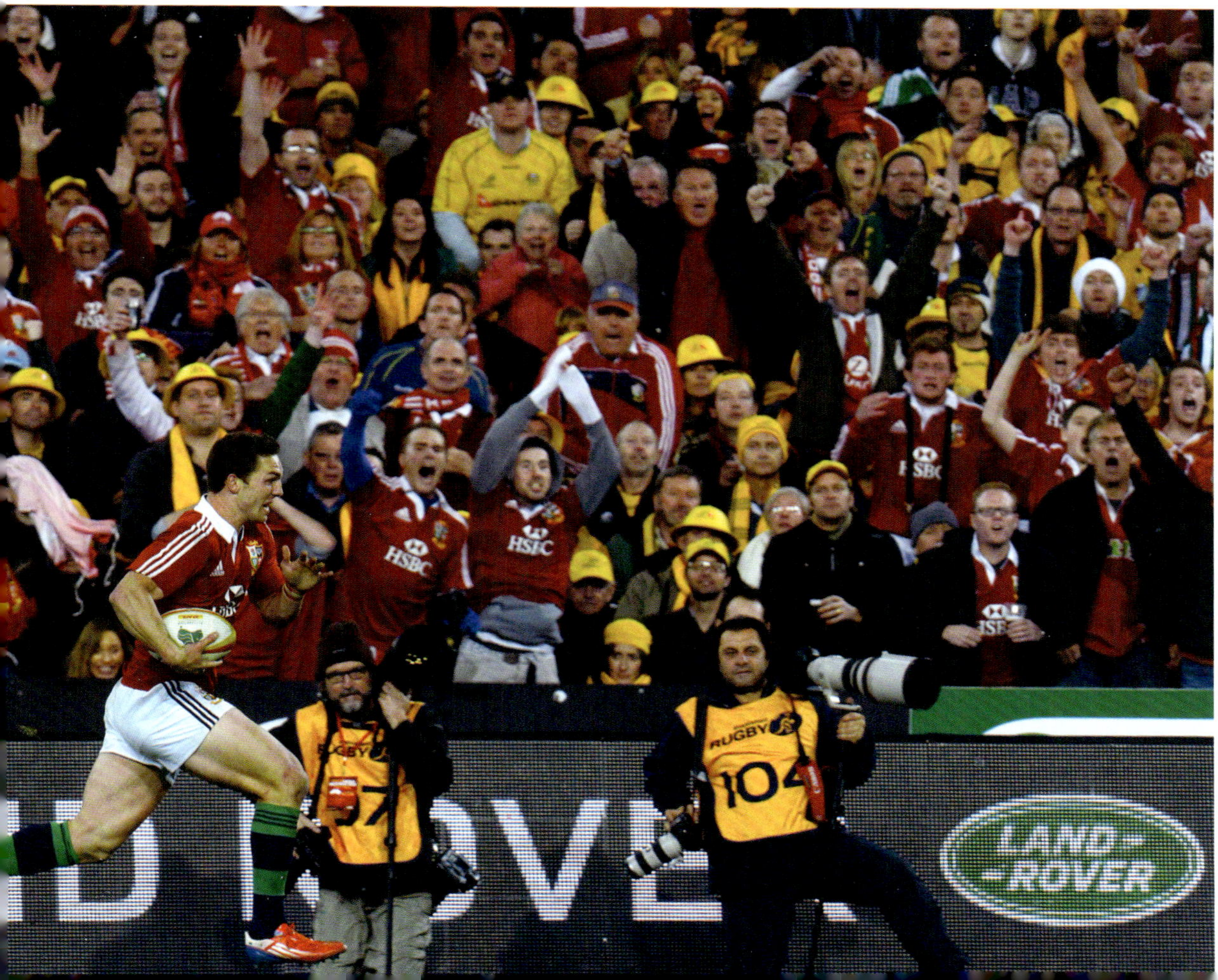
HSBC
RUGBY
104
LAND-ROVER

24th minute. The Wallaby looked shocked, his emotional state compounded when coach Robbie Deans substituted the prop with immediate effect once his ten minutes in the cooler had come to an end. Things were to get worse still. Three minutes after Australia were reduced to 14 men, wing Israel

Folau, the danger man in gold, went to field a kick behind him, turned and immediately felt his hamstring. Off he went too. The Lions had their

opponents on the ropes. Yet, typically, defiantly, Australia would not give in. The Lions led 19-3 after 25 minutes and were in total control.

Yet from deep within, Australia summoned reserves of strength. They came back at the Lions. Jesse Mogg of the Brumbies came on for Folau and immediately showed why he was so highly regarded. One big, slicing run upfield looked as if it might reap rich reward, only for Lions lock Geoff Parling to throw himself at Mogg's rear foot. He made contact, clipping the heel and down Mogg went. For that tap-tackle alone, Parling deserved his match fee.

The Wallabies kept pressing and got their due return right on the stroke of half-time, when James O'Connor jinked his way over. O'Connor is not everyone's favourite, either as a fly half or as a bloke who knows his responsibilities off-field. Yet he can play, perhaps not as a No. 10 orchestrator but as one with a bit of devil within him. It was not a good time to concede. The Lions had been dominant but only led by nine points at 19-10. Even that margin had gone down to three within five minutes of the restart, Leali'ifano knocking over two goals.

This was to be the time when we found out just how tightknit this Lions group were. All those weeks of training together, all those evenings bonding and building spirit, it came down to this. Did they have the resolve and the togetherness to get through this? No Warburton. No O'Connell. No O'Driscoll.

But they had each other. Men such as their captain of the day, Alun Wyn Jones, who put in a typically grafting shift. Toby Faletau at No. 8 – terrific. And as for Halfpenny, the little man just grew and grew. There was a danger that Halfpenny would be known only for his boot, an accolade he would not have sniffed at. But here, just when it was needed, he showed that his legs could be used for something other than swinging goalwards.

The Lions full back had a decisive hand in two of the three tries scored in an 11-minute spell midway through the half, a spree that caused delirium up in the stands and jubilation in the coaches' box.

● **LEFT** 68th minute. Just three minutes after George North's strike, Conor Murray's superbly weighted pass finds Jamie Roberts, who accelerates between Mike Hooper and Christian Leali'ifano to score.

125

THIRD TEST

If you are going to claim your first series victory in 16 years, it probably doesn't matter if it is a scruffy, lucky, last-ditch win, because the history books will record it come what may. But this was glorious, quite glorious, a vindication of all that had gone on in the weeks building to this point. The Lions insisted that they had come to play rugby, throwing that lazy southern stereotype of northern-hemisphere rugby being for dullards back in their faces.

Here was the proof.

George North, Jonathan Davies and Halfpenny did the work for Jonny Sexton's try in the 57th minute, a classy effort down the left flank. Eight minutes later, it was Halfpenny's scintillating run that paved the way for North. The Wallabies were wobbling. Moments later, they were on their backsides conceding an easy try to Jamie Roberts,

Halfpenny's conversion taking the score to 41-16 and into the realms of fantasy.

It was well and truly all over still with 11 minutes to run. The playing and coaching staff began gathering on the touch line long before the final whistle sounded. There were hugs and back-slaps, all thoroughly merited.

The 30,000 who had made the pilgrimage to Australia had seen their faith rewarded. Rumour has it that drink might have been taken that night, likewise in the Lions camp. All richly deserved.

Gatland had primed his men for this moment.

'We spoke about being prepared to go to a place that not many players go to in terms of pushing your body to the limit,' he said. 'We came out with the attitude that we wanted to play some rugby and move the ball. Four tries was a vindication of how well we've played overall on this tour. The scrum was brilliant. I thought Alex Corbisiero was man of the match. These guys have done themselves and the jersey proud.'

They had done just that. Chapeau!

● ABOVE No side in Sydney. The Lions triumph over the Wallabies 41-16 on the night and by two Tests to one.
● LEFT Sam Warburton holds aloft the Tom Richards Cup as his men celebrate their induction into the very select club of victorious Lions sides.

OPINION Match 10

WARREN GATLAND

The Lions head coach (who revealed he had considered resigning in the wake of 'vitriolic' criticism over the O'Driscoll affair) had this to say after the Lions win:

■ *'It was an outstanding performance. We started well, came under some pressure and bounced back. I said that Australia were desperate last week and brought all their emotions. We felt there was another step up we could bring and we showed that. We scored four fantastic tries …*

'We are not leaving until Tuesday and I hope the next 48 hours do not get out of hand.'

ALUN WYN JONES

The lock and Lions captain for the match commented:

■ *'We proved that despite talk of selection, the northern hemisphere is doing well. The scoreline reflects what we wanted to do. We wanted to win the collisions and the breakdown. It was going to come down to that. They*

came back at us at the start of the second half, but we came through and I thought the backs did pretty well.

'We've been going well in the scrum. We haven't quite got the change [favourable decisions] we wanted in the first two Tests, but that's credit to Australia. But now credit to the front row – the starters and the bench – for their consistency. I was feeling it with 20 minutes to go, but the bench carried me through.'

JONATHAN SEXTON

The Lions stand-off and scorer of the second try reflected:

■ *'You remember those scenes from '97 and to be a part of the next team to win a series is a dream come true. We wanted to attack, but we didn't really get the ball off first phase in the first couple of Tests.*

'We got a bit more tonight. The scrum was dominant and that gave us a lot of penalties. Scrum time is always important when Romain Poite is refereeing. That's where we built our foundations. The way we bounced back was outstanding.'

BRIAN O'DRISCOLL

Although not on the field for the final chapter, O'Driscoll at last had a Lions series win at the fourth attempt:

■ *'I'm absolutely delighted. It's been a rollercoaster week for me, and it was emotional today and not being there, but essentially it is about winning a series and being part of that. I will always have it on my CV.'*

JONATHAN DAVIES

The Lions No. 13 described the success:

■ *'An amazing feeling. The amount of work we have put in and the emotions we have had. I have enjoyed every second. We clicked today.'*

GEORGE NORTH

The wing, who scored two tries in the series, commented on the Lions performance:

■ *'Today we came out the way we wanted since the first game. After a long season and a long tour this is what we were after as a squad.'*

● **LEFT** Opposing skippers Alun Wyn Jones and James Horwill engage in aerial combat at the ANZ Stadium.

SAM WARBURTON

The tour captain explained that it had been a challenging set of Test matches:

■ *'The Australian boys made it very tough for us and it was an immense series.'*

JAMIE ROBERTS

The centre, restored to the ranks for the final Test, praised the team's approach:

■ *'The guys were really disciplined in attack and defence. It was clinical rugby. Our contact area was fantastic and the scrum was very dominant.'*

LEIGH HALFPENNY

The runaway man of the series was modest about his role:

■ *'The pack was outstanding. I dreamed of this my whole life. Winning man of the series is again a dream, but I could not have done it without the others.'*

ALEX CORBISIERO

The prop had refused to get carried away after his early try:

■ *'I'll take tries any time, but there was so much time to go that I had to try to stay focused and not lose my head. In the scrum we tried to put down a marker. The referee saw our dominance and gave us key penalties. It's already a career highlight … but to be continued. It shows me what I am capable of. It's been a tough year, but this is the perfect way to end it.'*

ROBBIE DEANS

The Wallaby coach explained what had gone wrong:

■ *'It was a horrific start. They used their set-piece to great advantage and fed off it. The Lions play the game in a very simple way and we needed to take them out of their comfort zone. They were turning the scoreboard over. And we really allowed them to thrive.*
'We just had to hold on to the ball, but we didn't. We let them execute the way they wanted and they scored points. It was disappointing in the scrum. We'd done so well in the first two Tests but we let ourselves down there.'

JAMES HORWILL

The Australia captain expressed pretty similar views:

■ *'We got penalised early and then got a bit gun shy. We sat on the back foot and allowed them to dictate. We just weren't good enough. In the end we dug deep and tried as hard as we could. You'd have to say the better team won. We just had to hold on to the ball and build pressure, but we didn't.'*

WILL GENIA

The live-wire scrum half knew he probably wouldn't get another go at the Lions:

■ *'They scored an early try and we're chasing the game right from the start. Obviously I'm gutted. You only get one shot at this, unless you are George Smith. We got it back to 19-16, and from then on it just went downhill. They put us to the sword. They scored a lot of tries.'*

● **ABOVE** George Smith, a Wallaby since 2000, owner of 111 Australia caps and, like Brian O'Driscoll, a survivor of the 2001 series, takes a look back as he leaves the field in Sydney.

GEORGE SMITH

Veteran flanker Smith was taken by surprise:

■ *'Obviously devastated. I didn't envisage this result.'*

And on his head clash with Richard Hibbard:

■ *'It obviously affected me. You saw me snake-dancing off the field. I passed the concussion tests, but the impact that I envisioned before the game didn't eventuate. That's my role – to disrupt play within that breakdown area. I don't think I did that.*
'I think it's time for the young guys who have been working hard within Australian rugby to have a chance.'

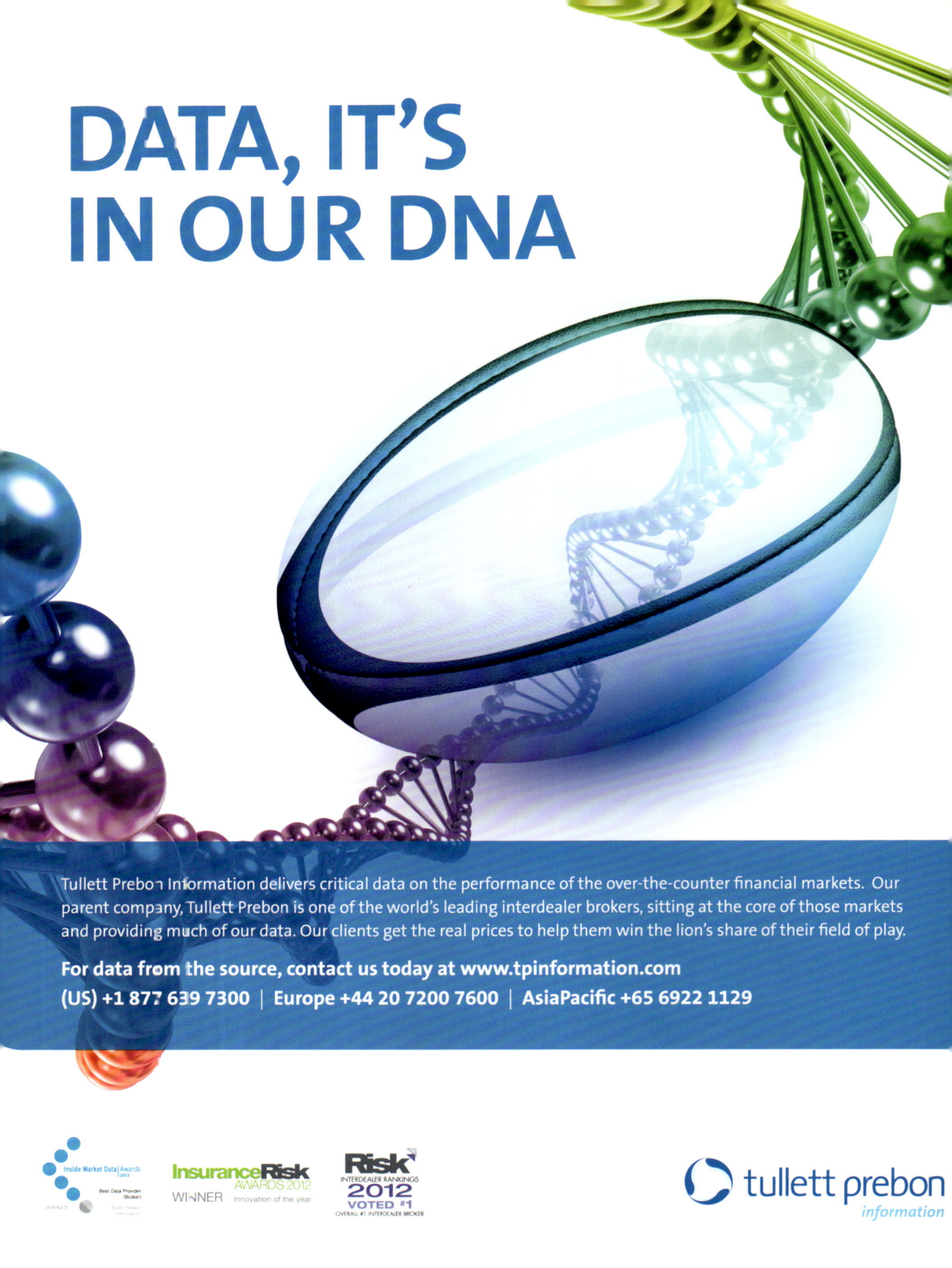

DATA, IT'S IN OUR DNA

Tullett Prebon Information delivers critical data on the performance of the over-the-counter financial markets. Our parent company, Tullett Prebon is one of the world's leading interdealer brokers, sitting at the core of those markets and providing much of our data. Our clients get the real prices to help them win the lion's share of their field of play.

For data from the source, contact us today at www.tpinformation.com

(US) +1 877 639 7300 | Europe +44 20 7200 7600 | AsiaPacific +65 6922 1129

tullett prebon
information

What Went Wrong for the Wallabies?

by Georgina Robinson of *The Sydney Morning Herald*

Hot with shame after a 33-6 shellacking at the hands of the mercurial French last November, Adam Ashley-Cooper stood against a wall in one of the anonymous function rooms inside London's Royal Garden Hotel and summed up everything right and wrong with Australian rugby in the current era.

'We let ourselves down last week. There were a lot of Australians who got up early to watch us back home, there were a lot of Australians that turned up at the Stade de France to watch us and we let them down, we let ourselves down,' Ashley-Cooper said.

'We want to respond. We're a pretty tight group, it's never going to be rosy and there's always going to be critics, it's just about getting on with it and, more than anything, using it as motivation.'

What didn't make the published version of those remarks, but is even more illustrative, was the Wallabies utility's use of the word 'mate' to punctuate every prickly response.

'We let ourselves down last week, mate.'

'We want to respond, mate.'

'Mate, we're a pretty tight group ...'

Mate, mate, mate. Two Australian journalists walked out of the hotel into the damp cold of late-autumn London that day knowing the Wallabies were warming themselves up for just the latest fightback performance of their 2012 season.

● **BELOW** The Lions run up against a wall of Aussie stubbornness in Melbourne as Adam Ashley-Cooper takes the game away from them with a 75th-minute try.

They beat England 20-14 the next day, with a triumphant scrum that boasted the same man at tight-head prop who was to shoulder much of the blame for Australia's loss to the Lions in Sydney eight months later.

So while it is tempting and in no small way accurate to blame the Wallabies' set-piece woes for their capitulation in the series decider, it is also all too easy. There were far more complex forces at play in the collective headspace of the Australian Test team. The Twickenham victory represents the best it can produce. The Sydney three-Test-series denouement, the worst.

As a starting point, consider this explanation from former Wallabies second-rower Nathan Sharpe, who captained Australia on that end-of-year tour before signing on as a line-out coach for the Lions series: 'We had to rely on emotion because we weren't consistent in our performance. Emotion was too much of a deciding factor in how the team actually played. We lost games that we should have won easily and we won games that we probably shouldn't have won, because we had been on that emotional rollercoaster.'

Sharpe made those comments two and a half weeks out from the first Test in Brisbane, while the Lions were testing combinations against weak opponents dotted around the lucky country and the Wallabies were bunkered down, testing no one but each other, on Queensland's Sunshine Coast.

'Sharpey', as Australians call him, knows a thing or two about the Wallabies mindset, having earned 116 Test caps during a thrilling 11-year international career. In what can only be described as Australian rugby's annus horribilis – a 2012 season that forced doomed coach Robbie Deans to cycle through four

captains, five half backs (scrum halves) and no less than 14 debutants as injury claimed all of his stars – Sharpe had no choice but to tap into that rich vein of 'Aussie battler' emotion. It saw him out of some tight spots, lifting the Wallabies to a six-point win against Argentina after a 31-8 bollocking on the highveld in the Rugby Championship, and to an 18-18 draw in the final Bledisloe Cup match after a 22-0 humiliation in the first.

It is in every way a classic Australian response. Need something done against the odds? Summon that deep fear of inadequacy, back yourself into a corner and fight as if your life depended on it.

The Lions were on the receiving end of that stubborn trait in the second Test in Melbourne. With everything on the line, the Wallabies refused to let the game go. Horwill shunned an easy penalty goal with less than ten minutes on the clock because he

knew nothing less than a converted try would take the team to Sydney – and he hadn't endured the vacillations of the International Rugby Board's judicial process for the series to end there, under the closed Etihad Stadium roof.

And so, against the odds, at the end of one of the most trying Test weeks in recent Wallaby history, five-eighth James O'Connor put his 4am burger-joint escapades behind him to put Ashley-Cooper into space past Lions centre Jonathan Davies. As they had done so many times a year earlier, the Wallabies lived to play another Test match.

And therein lies the rub. Addicted to the rollercoaster ride, bereft of consistency, the Wallabies bounce from loss to gutsy win. It was ever thus, or at least since the 2011 Rugby World Cup, where quarter-final survival against the Springboks barely atoned for a pool-stage loss to Ireland, before set-piece collapse sent them back across the Tasman Sea after a semi-final mauling from the All Blacks.

Is a pattern beginning to emerge? Victory in the second Test against the Lions threw the Wallabies a lifeline but robbed them of their go-to motivators.

Two days before the final Test at the ANZ Stadium, an uncharacteristically relaxed and communicative Deans sat in Sydney's Shangri-La Hotel and predicted his players were on the cusp of their 'best performance without a doubt'. One day before the final Test, the same confidence was exhibited in the body language and words of senior Wallabies Will Genia and Stephen Moore.

The same two journalists, the ones who left the Royal Garden Hotel last November sensing a comeback in the works, glanced at each other and knew. Somehow, despite a back line brimming with threats, a back row boasting unrivalled experience and a tight five that had finally thrown off the southern-hemisphere pretenders tag, the Wallabies were not out of the woods yet. The enemy was not George North, Jamie Roberts, Adam Jones or Alex Corbisiero, as powerful and clinical a performance as they would muster on the night. The enemy, for the Wallabies, was right between the ears. It would fell them at the kick-off.

● LEFT A relaxed-looking Robbie Deans with James Horwill and Kurtley Beale at the team photo on the eve of the third Test.

BRING ON THE BRITISH LIONS

THE REAL TEST IS IN 2017

The Odds Defied

They came to win, not merely to compete. The 2009 Lions tourists had restored pride in the jersey after the debacle of 2005. Warren Gatland's side had to go one better. And they did. That was the criterion by which they wanted to be judged. They did not want to attract sympathy for gallant failure. They had had enough of that. There was a fair amount of tosh spoken about the credibility of Lions tours being under threat if this tour had gone the way of the previous three and ended in defeat.

Of course, there would be questions raised and there would have to be a serious inquest as to whether the Lions could take on the southern giants in the modern era with restrictive preparation time. Those questions remain valid. Let us hope they carry more, and not less, force now that Gatland's men have laid the bogey to rest.

But it was absurd to suggest that the public would fall out of love with the Lions. They came in their many thousands to Australia, fuelled by their love of romance and tradition. They know that it is tough, nigh on impossible, to blend four into one in the space of a few weeks. It was always a difficult task. In the modern era, when attacks as well as defences are so choreographed, it has become even

● **ABOVE** Within touching distance now. Jamie Roberts accepts the plaudits from his team-mates after delivering the coup de grâce with his try in the third Test at Sydney.

more of an improbable labour. The degree of understanding required is so acute, so complex, that to make it happen requires ingenuity on the part of the coaches as well as selflessness of each and every player. That is exactly what occurred on this trip.

The Lions did not field the same line-up once in ten matches. Only six players started all three Tests. Some of that was due to choice by the coaches; some of it down to injury. The Lions lost two captains – Sam Warburton and the 2009 leader, Paul O'Connell – to injury and chose to leave out another, Brian O'Driscoll. All that alone makes for an unsettled feel. Yet still the Lions managed to play with a greater degree of unity and cohesion than the Wallabies, who had been in camp for three weeks prior to the series and had spent countless more hours on the training field over the preceding couple of years.

How then is it possible to defy the natural process? Setting the tone is key. Sir Ian McGeechan in tandem with tour manager Gerald Davies did much to restore values on the 2009 South Africa trip. They recognised that the Lions cannot hope to match their opponents' degree of preparation and familiarity. They have to make up for that shortfall by appealing to the players' sense of the moment, to get them to recognise what the possibilities are. Trust is of paramount importance. That is why players share rooms. That is why the midweek side is as valued as the Saturday side. In fact, on this tour, there was no difference whatsoever right up until the first Test, with Gatland insisting that every

player had a legitimate crack at that Test jersey. Every coach will spout that maxim – although Graham Henry was to stray from the 'one for all' ethos in 2001 – but the players have to see at close quarters that it is actually true. If it is, and it was here, then training becomes more competitive and standards rise accordingly.

Gatland was as good as his word. How could it not have been so? This was the man who had passed over one of his closest friends, Shaun Edwards, in favour of another former Wigan great, Andy Farrell, because he believed that Farrell would bring more out of him as a coach for the simple reason that he was an unknown quantity. It would take Gatland out of his comfort zone. The players were all too aware of how much sacrifice that entailed. That is why when it came to the Brian O'Driscoll decision, you knew that it had been made in good faith. You may not have agreed with it. But you could respect it.

● **BELOW Tour** captain Sam Warburton in action during the second Test in Melbourne before his hamstring injury. The Lions had already lost 2009 skipper Paul O'Connell and chose not to select 2005 captain Brian O'Driscoll (left) for the third Test.
● FACING PAGE Warren Gatland chose England backs coach Andy Farrell to take charge of the Lions' defence.

These Lions all bought in to the philosophy. The modern player tends to have everything laid on for him. The Lion has to put up with a less pampered existence. He is expected to muck in, to back up Saturday to Wednesday and still train with intensity. In truth, that is what the players want. They want the experience to be testing. They want it to be different, challenging. That is what makes it special.

Of course, administrators should do all that they can to ensure that the tourists leave these shores in as good a condition as the system allows. As things stand, the system allows for precious little.

It is scandalous that for an event which creates so much excitement in the rugby community more slack is not created in the season's structure. The 2013 Lions were given nothing by the respective organisers of the Aviva, Rabo and European competitions. Fourteen players involved in the various finals only met their new mates a few hours before leaving Heathrow. Crazy.

The 2013 Lions manager, Andy Irvine, despaired. He believed that little could be done for the 2017 tour to New Zealand, but that once existing contracts came to an end just after that, changes should be made.

'The one thing I would say – and I passionately believe in this – is that the scheduling is all wrong,' said Irvine, speaking from a position of strength in victory rather than being accused of sour grapes. 'We as a board did our damnedest to give Warren more time. It is absolutely bonkers that you have a Rabo final and an Aviva final 48 hours before you fly out. Believe me, we tried as hard as we could to change that. I am not sure if we can change it in four years' time, but thereafter, once the SANZAR agreement [the touring deal between the Lions and Australia, New Zealand and South Africa] comes up for negotiation, make no mistake, our boys will get more time with the players. They have to, because it is unfair on the coaches and the players. There is a legally binding contract in place. Unless both parties agree to changing that contract, you can't break it. We are powerless to break it, unless we have the agreement of the New Zealand Rugby Union or, alternatively, the clubs back home. You try to persuade the Premiership clubs to move their final, or try to persuade ERC [European Rugby Cup] to

move their final. If you can do it, you are a better man than me. We can't force them to do it. We've offered them money and tried to impress upon them how important Lions tours are. What we did this year was give the lads an extra two weeks' training, and only the ones involved in the two finals didn't attend training. That was 13 or 14 of them, but Gats would tell you that the preparation this time was better than it was in 2009.'

It was an impassioned plea for more help to be given to the cause. Regrettably, it is likely to fall on stony ground. Vested interest rules the roost. Moreover, you can hear the bleating across the committee-room table now: 'If Gatland's men managed to achieve a record victory over Australia, then why is more preparation time needed?'

The answer is that they did it in spite of the system rather than because of it. It also has to be noted that this was a pretty ordinary Wallaby time, the 2013 Australians nowhere near as strong as either the 2001 or 1989 sides. If the Lions had fallen here, then there really would not have been much hope. Australia had potential in their back line, no more than a decent smattering of talent in their forward pack, but precious little else. Players such as Genia, Folau, Beale and O'Connor have bags of talent, but harnessing it all is something else. That was obviously the view of the Australian union, who saw fit to get rid of head coach Robbie Deans immediately after the series finished. The New Zealander was replaced by Ewen McKenzie, a supporter of mercurial fly half Quade Cooper. What might have been, eh?

The Lions cast nary a backward glance at the fallout from the series. It would be 12 years before they visited again. McKenzie would not still be in post by then, nor many, if any, of the players.

But the Lions were different. Even though their narrative came to an end with the final whistle in Sydney, thoughts were already turning to 2017 and the trip to New Zealand, the most arduous of tours. Gatland was asked if he fancied another crack at it himself and could not conceal his desire to take a

● FACING PAGE Will Genia gets the ball away during the Melbourne Test. The Wallabies were not as strong as in 2001 and 1989, though Genia and several other backs had 'bags of talent'.

● ABOVE **Stuart Hogg takes on Rod Davies of the Queensland Reds in Brisbane. The Scotland full back was among a group of young Lions who could form the core of the 2017 touring party to New Zealand.**
● FACING PAGE **Standing tall. Toby Faletau, who started at No. 8 in the third Test in Sydney and had a storming game.**

Lions side to the land of his birth. He was steeped in the tradition of the Lions tourists and had played against them for Waikato in 1993. The Wales coach, though, is keenly aware of the fickleness of his trade. Who knows? Perhaps he might even be All Blacks coach by then!

What is clear is that this trip has seen the nurturing of young players who will be in their prime in 2017. There is a raft of youngsters such as George North, Alex Cuthbert, Manu Tuilagi, Owen Farrell, Stuart Hogg and Toby Faletau – all of whom have benefited from this experience. They will be the nucleus of the Lions in four years' time. Many feel that taking on the All Blacks is mission impossible in this age. These players would beg to differ.

Gatland would certainly agree with them.

'If you look at how young this squad is, a lot of them could be around in four years' time,' said Gatland. 'That potentially makes the Lions squad in four years' time incredibly strong. That is something to be excited about.'

Gatland also agreed with his manager that more needed to be done to offset the difficulties of preparation. He had deliberately taken a compact squad, figuring that the upside of giving everyone an even chance to start outweighed the benefits of having cover for injury and fatigue. Gatland revised that view during the trip, wondering if you might need to look at squad numbers in the region of 42-44. Mind you, so much is down to good fortune. The Lions were reduced to 11 or 12 backs at training in mid-tour, yet had 19 available for the final week.

Gatland handled all these issues well. He is something of a gunslinger is Gatland, happiest when the bullets are firing. But even he was taken aback by the level of abuse he received in the wake of dropping O'Driscoll. Extraordinarily, he did not feel able to take any satisfaction in the immediate aftermath of victory. 'I was absolutely shocked by what was said,' said the coach in the bowels of the ANZ Stadium site as thousands celebrated outside. 'It was vitriolic. I haven't taken a lot of pleasure out of this in terms of feeling vindicated. I haven't enjoyed the last 72 hours, it's been tough personally.'

In some ways, the outpouring was a back-handed compliment. People care about the Lions. The widespread response illustrated that – even if it did stray into the realms of sordid invective. That, sadly, is a reality of social media, which gives free rein to cowards with keyboards. You might imagine that they would think twice about saying it to the man's face.

Gatland dealt well with all manner of things. There are rough edges to him. He likes to socialise but cuts the same slack to his players. He is a grown-up and expects others to be too. When it is time to be serious, he is very serious. He is old school in that regard. He trusts players to do the right thing. That faith was repaid.

● **ABOVE** Lions head coach Warren Gatland disappears in to the tunnel at the ANZ Stadium after his side had despatched Australia 41-16 and lifted the Tom Richards Cup.
● **RIGHT** Not just bish-bosh. Jonathan Davies makes the crucial break in the move by the Lions back line that resulted in Jonathan Sexton's try in the third Test in Sydney.

He got his coaching team on the right wavelength and there was far more subtlety in the Lions attacking strategy than was depicted, as if it were no more than bish-bosh 'Warrenball' rugby based around huge backs piling forward. There is nothing wrong with such an approach, but a glance at the three tries scored in the second-half in Sydney tells you that there is brain to go with that brawn.

Several players left Australia with enhanced reputations – Leigh Halfpenny, George North, Jonathan Davies, Alex Corbisiero, Alun Wyn Jones, Adam Jones – and many more can hold their heads high too. They were a credit to themselves. The Lions came to Australia determined to restore a sense of glory to the jersey. They did just that.

Fig. 1: *Typical British and Irish Profits (hoping for some tries)*

Discipline, intense concentration and effort – sound familiar? All these elements are just as important on the Profit hunting ground as they are on the rugby pitch.

If you'd like to find out more about Hunting Profits please contact your financial adviser, call 0800 092 2051 or visit artemis.co.uk.

ARTEMIS
The PROFIT Hunter

The value of an investment, and any income from it, can fall as well as rise as a result of market and currency fluctuations and you may not get back the amount originally invested. Please remember that past performance is not a guide to the future.

Issued by Artemis Fund Managers Ltd which is authorised and regulated by the Financial Conduct Authority (www.fca.org.uk), 25 The North Colonnade, Canary Wharf, London E14 5HS.

TOUR STATISTICS

SATURDAY 1 JUNE HONG KONG STADIUM, HONG KONG
British & Irish Lions 59 Barbarians 8
(HALF-TIME 23-3)

● **Barbarians:** J Payne; J Rokocoko, E Daly, C Laulala, T Ngwenya; N Evans, D Yachvili; P James, S Brits, M Castrogiovanni; M Wentzel, D Mumm; S Manoa, S Jones, S Parisse (c)
REPLACEMENTS: L Ghiraldini for Manoa 10-19 (temp), for Brits 45; D Jones for James 58; A Lo Cicero for Castrogiovanni 69; J Hamilton for Wentzel 59; I Harinordoquy for Jones 53; K Fotuali'i for Yachvili 53; J Hook for Laulala 68; M Tindall for Ngwenya 60
SCORERS: Try – Fotuali'i; Penalty – Daly

● **British & Irish Lions:** S Hogg; A Cuthbert, J Davies, J Roberts, S Maitland; O Farrell, M Phillips; M Vunipola, R Hibbard, A Jones; R Gray, P O'Connell (c); D Lydiate, J Tipuric, T Faletau
REPLACEMENTS: T Youngs for Hibbard 43; C Healy for Vunipola 55; M Stevens for A Jones 55; AW Jones for O'Connell 29-36 (blood), 62; J Heaslip for Faletau 62; C Murray for Phillips 57; J Sexton for Farrell 57; G North for Roberts 67
SCORERS: Tries – O'Connell, Phillips (2), Davies, Cuthbert (2), Lydiate, AW Jones; Conversions – Farrell (3), Sexton (2); Penalties – Farrell (3)

YELLOW CARD Brits (Barbarians) 7
REFEREE Steve Walsh (Australia)
ATTENDANCE 28,643

WEDNESDAY 5 JUNE PATERSONS STADIUM, PERTH
Western Force 17 British & Irish Lions 69
(HALF-TIME 3-27)

● **Western Force:** S Christie; D Haylett-Petty, E Stubbs, C Tuatara-Morrison, C Brown; S Norton-Knight, B Sheehan; S Manu, J Hilterbrand, S Ma'afu; T Lynn, P Battye; A Cottrell, M Hodgson (c), R Brown
REPLACEMENTS: H Roach for Hilterbrand 78; S Kolo for Ma'afu 49; T Metcher for Manu 77; B Matwijow for Lynn 65; L McCaffrey for Cottrell 52; A Mathewson for Sheehan 71; N Haining for Brown 6; J Rasolea for Haylett-Petty 71
SCORERS: Tries – Brown, McCaffrey; Conversions – Sheehan (2); Penalty – Sheehan

● **British & Irish Lions:** L Halfpenny; T Bowe, B O'Driscoll (c), M Tuilagi, G North; J Sexton, C Murray; C Healy, R Best, D Cole; AW Jones, I Evans; T Croft, S O'Brien, J Heaslip
REPLACEMENTS: T Youngs for Best 59; M Vunipola for Healy 37; M Stevens for Cole 68; G Parling for Evans 59; T Faletau for Croft 71; B Youngs for Murray 66; O Farrell for Sexton 66; S Maitland for Bowe 76
SCORERS: Tries – Sexton, O'Driscoll (2), Croft, Heaslip, Vunipola, Bowe, Farrell, Parling; Conversions – Halfpenny (9); Penalties – Halfpenny (2)

YELLOW CARDS Stubbs (Force) 57, AW Jones (Lions) 71
REFEREE Glen Jackson (New Zealand)
ATTENDANCE 35,103

SATURDAY 8 JUNE SUNCORP STADIUM, BRISBANE
Queensland Reds 12 British & Irish Lions 22
(HALF-TIME 7-16)

● **Queensland Reds:** B Lucas; R Davies, B Tapuai, A Fainga'a, L Morahan; Q Cooper (c), N Frisby; B Daley, J Hanson, G Holmes; E O'Donoghue, A Wallace-Harrison; E Quirk, B Robinson, J Schatz
REPLACEMENTS: A Anae for Daley 24; S Denny for Anae 78; J Owen for Holmes 36-40 (blood), 69; R Samo for O'Donoghue 12-19 (blood), for Wallace-Harrison 55; J Butler for Robinson 55; J Lance for Frisby 68; Frisby for Lucas 70; M Harris for Fainga'a 53; D Shipperley for Morahan 44
SCORERS: Tries – Morahan, Frisby; Conversion – Cooper

● **British & Irish Lions:** S Hogg; A Cuthbert, M Tuilagi, J Davies, T Bowe; O Farrell, B Youngs; M Vunipola, T Youngs, M Stevens; R Gray, G Parling; D Lydiate, S Warburton (c), T Faletau
REPLACEMENTS: R Hibbard for T Youngs 64; D Cole for Vunipola 64; A Jones for Stevens 64; P O'Connell for Gray 64; J Tipuric for Warburton 74; C Murray; J Sexton for Bowe 46; G North for Tuilagi 20
SCORERS: Try – B Youngs; Conversion – Farrell; Penalties – Farrell (5)

REFEREE Jérôme Garcès (France)
ATTENDANCE 50,136

TUESDAY 11 JUNE HUNTER STADIUM, NEWCASTLE
Combined Country 0 British & Irish Lions 64
(HALF-TIME 0-38)

● **Combined NSW-QLD Country:** N Trist; A Gibbon, L Catt, T-J Siakisini, T Cox; A Roberts, M Snowden; H Hirsimaki, J Mann-Rea, T Metcher; P Battye, B Enever; R Stanford, J Butler, T Davidson (c)
REPLACEMENTS: T Kearney for Mann-Rea 61; D Evans for Hirsimaki 53; R Abraham for Metcher 68; R Arnold for Stanford 72; T Dyer for Battye 50; A McCormack for Snowden 72; S McCarthy for Cox 57; D Ah-Wang for Catt 62

● **British & Irish Lions:** S Maitland; A Cuthbert, B O'Driscoll (c), J Roberts, G North; S Hogg, C Murray; A Corbisiero, R Hibbard, D Cole; R Gray, I Evans; S O'Brien, J Tipuric, J Heaslip
REPLACEMENTS: R Best for Hibbard 50; R Grant for Corbisiero 50; M Stevens for Cole 50; AW Jones for Gray 41; T Faletau for Heaslip 54; M Phillips for Murray 70; J Davies for Roberts 55; L Halfpenny for North 41
SCORERS: Tries – Cuthbert, Murray, Hogg, North (2), Hibbard, O'Driscoll, Halfpenny, O'Brien, Davies; Conversions – Hogg (4), Halfpenny (3)

REFEREE Steve Walsh (Australia)
ATTENDANCE 20,071

SATURDAY 15 JUNE ALLIANZ STADIUM, SYDNEY
NSW Waratahs 17 British & Irish Lions 47
(HALF-TIME 10-23)

● **NSW Waratahs:** D Mitchell; C Crawford, R Horne, T Carter, P Betham; B Foley, B McKibbin; J Tilse, J Ulugia, P Ryan; W Skelton, O Atkins; J Holloway, P McCutcheon, D Dennis (c)
REPLACEMENTS: L Holmes for Ulugia 72; R Aho for Tilse 72; S Talakai for Ryan 72; L Timani for Holloway 49; A Gilbert for McCutcheon 55; M Lucas for McKibbin 72; B Volavola for Betham 72; T Kingston for Carter 46
SCORERS: Tries – Carter (2); Conversions – McKibbin (2); Penalty – McKibbin

● **British & Irish Lions:** L Halfpenny; S Maitland, J Davies, J Roberts, S Zebo; J Sexton, M Phillips; M Vunipola, T Youngs, A Jones; AW Jones, P O'Connell; T Croft, S Warburton (c), J Heaslip
REPLACEMENTS: R Hibbard for T Youngs 59; A Corbisiero for Vunipola 59; D Cole for A Jones 59; G Parling for O'Connell 59; D Lydiate for Croft 59; B Youngs for Phillips 59; O Farrell for Sexton 49; R Kearney for Halfpenny 59
SCORERS: Tries – Sexton, Halfpenny (2), Croft, Davies; Conversions – Halfpenny (4), Farrell; Penalties – Halfpenny (4)

REFEREE Jaco Peyper (South Africa)
ATTENDANCE 40,805

TUESDAY 18 JUNE CANBERRA STADIUM, CANBERRA
Brumbies 14 British & Irish Lions 12
(HALF-TIME 8-3)

● **Brumbies:** J Mogg; H Speight, T Kuridrani, A Smith, C Rathbone; M Toomua, I Prior; S Sio, S Siliva, R Smith; L Power, S Carter; S Fardy, C Fainga'a, P Kimlin (c)
REPLACEMENTS: J Mann-Rea for Siliva 57; J-P Smith; C Cocca; E Oosthuizen for Power 76; J Smiler for Carter 67; M Swanepoel; R Coleman for Rathbone 72; Z Holmes for A Smith 76
SCORERS: Try – Kuridrani; Penalties – Mogg (3)

● **British & Irish Lions:** R Kearney; C Wade, B Barritt, B Twelvetrees, S Williams; S Hogg, B Youngs; R Grant, R Best (c), M Stevens; R Gray, I Evans; S O'Brien, J Tipuric, T Faletau
REPLACEMENTS: R Hibbard for Best 57; A Corbisiero for Grant 57; D Cole for Stevens 57; G Parling for Evans 60; D Lydiate for O'Brien 57; C Murray for Youngs 60; O Farrell for Hogg 60; S Zebo for Williams 69
SCORERS: Penalties – Hogg (2), Farrell (2)

REFEREE Jérôme Garcès (France)
ATTENDANCE 21,655

SATURDAY 22 JUNE SUNCORP STADIUM, BRISBANE
Australia 21 British & Irish Lions 23
(HALF-TIME 12-13)

● **Australia:** B Barnes; I Folau, A Ashley-Cooper, C Leali'ifano, D Ioane; J O'Connor, W Genia; B Robinson, S Moore, B Alexander; K Douglas, J Horwill (c); B Mowen, M Hooper, W Palu
REPLACEMENTS: S Fainga'a; J Slipper for Robinson 68; S Kepu for Alexander 58; R Simmons for Douglas 68; L Gill for McCabe 47; N Phipps for Ashley-Cooper 77; P McCabe for Leali'ifano 2; K Beale for Barnes 38
SCORERS: Tries – Folau (2); Conversion – O'Connor; Penalties – O'Connor, Beale (2)

● **British & Irish Lions:** L Halfpenny; A Cuthbert, B O'Driscoll, J Davies, G North; J Sexton, M Phillips; A Corbisiero, T Youngs, A Jones; AW Jones, P O'Connell; T Croft, S Warburton (c), J Heaslip
REPLACEMENTS: R Hibbard for T Youngs 65; M Vunipola for Corbisiero 52; D Cole for A Jones 52; G Parling for AW Jones 70; D Lydiate for Croft 73; B Youngs for Phillips 62; O Farrell; S Maitland
SCORERS: Tries – North, Cuthbert; Conversions – Halfpenny (2); Penalties – Halfpenny (3)

REFEREE Chris Pollock (New Zealand)
ATTENDANCE 52,499

TUESDAY 25 JUNE AAMI PARK, MELBOURNE
Melbourne Rebels 0 British & Irish Lions 35
(HALF-TIME 0-14)

● **Melbourne Rebels:** J Woodward; T English, M Inman, R Sidey, L Mitchell; B Hegarty, L Burgess; N Henderson, G Robinson, L Weeks; H Pyle, C Neville; J Saffy, S Fuglistaller, G Delve (c)
REPLACEMENTS: P Leafa for Robinson 61; P Alo-Emile for Weeks 61; C Ah-Nau for Henderson 61; L Jones for Pyle 41; J Reid for Delve 56; N Stirzaker for Burgess 56; A Roberts for Hegarty 72; C Vuna for Inman 50

● **British & Irish Lions:** R Kearney; S Maitland, M Tuilagi, B Barritt, S Zebo; O Farrell, C Murray; R Grant, R Hibbard, D Cole; R Gray, I Evans; D Lydiate (c), S O'Brien, T Faletau
REPLACEMENTS: R Best for Hibbard 55; T Court for Grant 55; M Stevens for Cole 55; T Croft for Lydiate 64; J Tipuric for O'Brien 55; B Youngs for Murray 62; B Twelvetrees for Barritt 32-40 (blood), for Kearney 62; S Hogg for Farrell 52
SCORERS: Tries – Murray, Maitland, O'Brien, penalty, Youngs; Conversions – Farrell (3), Hogg (2)

YELLOW CARD Reid (Rebels) 64
REFEREE Glen Jackson (New Zealand)
ATTENDANCE 28,648

SATURDAY 29 JUNE ETIHAD STADIUM, MELBOURNE
Australia 16 British & Irish Lions 15
(HALF-TIME 9-12)

● **Australia:** K Beale; I Folau, A Ashley-Cooper, C Leali'ifano, J Tomane; J O'Connor, W Genia; B Robinson, S Moore, B Alexander; K Douglas, J Horwill (c); B Mowen, M Hooper, W Palu
REPLACEMENTS: S Fainga'a; J Slipper for Robinson 60; S Kepu for Alexander 58; R Simmons for Douglas 53; L Gill for Palu 60; N Phipps; R Horne for Ashley-Cooper 79; J Mogg
SCORERS: Try – Ashley-Cooper; Conversion – Leali'ifano; Penalties – Leali'ifano (3)

● **British & Irish Lions:** L Halfpenny; T Bowe, B O'Driscoll, J Davies, G North; J Sexton, B Youngs; M Vunipola, T Youngs, A Jones; AW Jones, G Parling; D Lydiate, S Warburton (c), J Heaslip
REPLACEMENTS: R Hibbard for T Youngs 56; R Grant; D Cole for A Jones 58; T Croft for Warburton 66; S O'Brien for Heaslip 62; C Murray for B Youngs 53; O Farrell; A Cuthbert
SCORERS: Penalties – Halfpenny (5)

REFEREE Craig Joubert (South Africa)
ATTENDANCE 56,771

SATURDAY 6 JULY ANZ STADIUM, SYDNEY
Australia 16 British & Irish Lions 41
(HALF TIME 10-19)

● **Australia:** K Beale; I Folau, A Ashley-Cooper, C Leali'ifano, J Tomane; J O'Connor, W Genia; B Robinson, S Moore, B Alexander; K Douglas, J Horwill (c); B Mowen, G Smith, W Palu
REPLACEMENTS: S Fainga'a for Moore 55-62 (blood), 72; J Slipper for Robinson 66; S Kepu for Smith 26-36 (temp), for Alexander 36; R Simmons for Douglas 62; B McCalman for Palu 60; M Hooper for Smith 5-10 (temp), 66; N Phipps for Genia 69; J Mogg for Folau 27
SCORERS: Try – O'Connor; Conversion – Leali'ifano; Penalties – Leali'ifano (3)

● **British & Irish Lions:** L Halfpenny; T Bowe, J Davies, J Roberts, G North; J Sexton, M Phillips; A Corbisiero, R Hibbard, A Jones; AW Jones (c), G Parling; D Lydiate, S O'Brien, T Faletau
REPLACEMENTS: T Youngs for Hibbard 48; M Vunipola for Corbisiero 67; D Cole for A Jones 55; R Gray for Parling 68; J Tipuric for Faletau 55-59 (blood), for O'Brien 60; C Murray for Phillips 51; O Farrell for Sexton 64; M Tuilagi for Roberts 69
SCORERS: Tries – Corbisiero, Sexton, North, Roberts Conversions – Halfpenny (3); Penalties – Halfpenny (5)

YELLOW CARD Alexander (Australia) 24
REFEREE Romain Poite (France)
ATTENDANCE 83,702

■ TOP Leigh Halfpenny, Player of the Series and Lions top points scorer on tour with 114 points.
■ ABOVE George North, joint top try scorer for the tour with Alex Cuthbert, talks to tour manager Andy Irvine after the third Test.
■ FACING PAGE Tour captain Sam Warburton and third Test captain Alun Wyn Jones raise the Tom Richards Cup.

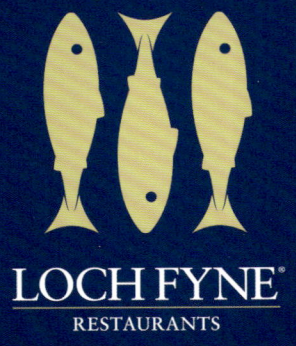

LOCH FYNE®
RESTAURANTS

"We started life as a small shack selling oysters on Scotland's West Highland route at the head of Loch Fyne. Our fish is sustainably sourced, either from abundant wild stocks or responsibly farmed"

- 42 restaurants nationwide, most of which are in unique historic or listed buildings

- A la carte menu with a wide range of fresh seafood and fish including our famous oysters and platters plus meat and vegetarian options

- Set menu available during daytime with 2 courses for £9.95

- Range of quality wines by the glass or bottle, selected by our Master wine buyer to complement our dishes

- Fresh fish and seafood available from our cold counter for you to purchase to cook at home

to find your local restaurant, view our menus or book a table, visit
www.lochfyne-restaurants.com

TOUR SUMMARY

APPEARANCES

NAME	ALL MATCHES	TESTS
Brad Barritt	2	
Rory Best	2+2	
Tommy Bowe	4	1
Dan Cole	3+6	0+3
Alex Corbisiero	3+2	2
Tom Court	0+1	
Tom Croft	3+2	1+1
Alex Cuthbert	4	1
Jonathan Davies	6+1	3
Ian Evans	4	
Toby Faletau	5+2	1
Owen Farrell	3+4	0+1
Ryan Grant	2+1	
Richie Gray	5+1	0+1
Leigh Halfpenny	5+1	3
Jamie Heaslip	5+1	2
Richard Hibbard	4+5	1+2
Stuart Hogg	4+1	
Adam Jones	5+1	3
Alun Wyn Jones	5+2	3
Rob Kearney	2+1	
Dan Lydiate	5+3	1+1

NAME	ALL MATCHES	TESTS
Sean Maitland	4+1	
Conor Murray	3+4	0+2
George North	5+2	3
Sean O'Brien	5+1	1+1
Paul O'Connell	3+1	1
Brian O'Driscoll	4	2
Geoff Parling	3+4	2+1
Mike Phillips	4+1	2
Jamie Roberts	4	1
Jonathan Sexton	5+2	3
Matt Stevens	2+4	
Justin Tipuric	3+3	0+1
Manu Tuilagi	3+1	0+1
Billy Twelvetrees	1+1	
Mako Vunipola	4+3	1+2
Christian Wade	1	
Sam Warburton	4	2
Shane Williams	1	
Ben Youngs	3+4	1+1
Tom Youngs	4+3	2+1
Simon Zebo	2+1	

(STARTS + REPLACEMENT APPEARANCES)

TRIES

4 A Cuthbert, G North

3 J Davies, L Halfpenny, B O'Driscoll, J Sexton

2 T Croft, C Murray, S O'Brien, M Phillips, B Youngs

1 T Bowe, A Corbisiero, O Farrell, R Hibbard, S Hogg, AW Jones, D Lydiate, S Maitland, P O'Connell, G Parling, J Roberts, M Vunipola

KICKERS

	PEN	CON	DG	PTS
L Halfpenny	19	21		99
O Farrell	10	8		46
S Hogg	2	6		18
J Sexton		2		4